Life Stories

Educator, Painter, Pilot, Stained-Glass Artist

From the Canady Photo Collection

Dr. Bob Canady created this firescreen.

Life Stories

Educator, Painter, Pilot, Stained-Glass Artist

Dr. Robert Canady

Copyright 2024 Dr. Robert Canady

All rights reserved. No part of this book may be reproduced or utilized in any form or by any means, electronic or mechanical, including photocopy, recording, or by an information storage and retrieval system, without permission in writing from the publisher.

Library of Congress Cataloging-in-Publication Data

ISBN: 979-8-9888614-5-4

Printed and bound in the United States of America by Ingram Lightning Source
First edition

Cover image: From Dr. Canady's firescreen panels
Cover design: Jacque Hillman
Editing, layout, and design: Jacque Hillman and Katie Gould

Photos are used in this book with permission granted from the photographer or organization, and the Canady Photo Collection includes Dr. Robert Canady's personal acquisitions and memorabilia from his past. Many stained-glass images in this book are from a 1990s church video.

The HillHelen Group LLC
470 North Parkway, Suite C
Jackson, TN 38305

The HillHelen Group LLC
635 North 65th Place
Mesa, AZ 85205

(731) 394-2894
www.hillhelengrouppublishers.com
hillhelengroup@gmail.com

High praise for *Life Stories*

"Bob Canady did the unthinkable! He brought the image of God's Word into a sanctuary of dark, wooden walls and illuminated it so that no one missed it. Eyes widened, jaws dropped, and words of praise were spoken. Yet Bob always deflected to the Lord, who showed him the way through the storm. Truly, God was glorified."
—*Rev. Don Dilday, former pastor of Trinity Hill United Methodist Church, Lexington, Kentucky*

"There are many talented artists in the world, but then there are others who are a cut above, those who touch the heart because the heart of the artist is so embedded in their work. You are in that top class of artists who create from their soul. What a joy to know your work and know your heart."
—*Sheila Hall, staff member, University of Memphis*

"Dr. Bob's kindness toward various churches in the region was welcomed with open arms, regardless of denomination or community. His lovely and supportive wife, Dr. Shirley Raines, was there all the way showing her support for the stained-glass windows projects. Each of them expressed their kindness, love, and support for each church, regardless of its design or denomination. Church members expressed gratitude for the generosity of this awesome team, for their commitment to the community."
—*Mark Stansbury, executive assistant for community relations, President's Office, University of Memphis*

"During a difficult time in my life, Bob created a beautiful stained-glass lamp for me as a way of expressing his love and concern. His passion and compassion for life and the people he cares about will always be evident in his marvelous art."
—*Dr. Ann Brown, MD*

"Bob is a true Renaissance man. He has been creative in so many aspects of his life: a problem solver, an artist, a vintage car restorer, an accomplished pilot, an adored professor, and a gifted storyteller. His life has been filled with adventure and creative accomplishments."
—*Dr. Rebecca Isbell, professor emerita, international speaker, and author*

"I remember how Dr. Bob listened to our ideas, and he heard what we wanted and was able to create that for us. Looking at it every Sunday is an inspiration."
—*Alandria London, church member, Freedom's Chapel Christian Church*

"I remember the children telling him they would like to see lots of colors when he asked what they wanted to see in the stained glass."
—*Linda Walker, church member, Freedom's Chapel Christian Church*

"Hearing Bob tell of his experience on that plane and his dedication to give back is always a reminder to me of the awesomeness one feels when they give back!"
—*Barbara H. Cole, church member, Freedom's Chapel Christian Church*

"We were approaching our anniversary, and the building's commercial glass windows, and the view outside them, were unattractive at best. Dr. Bob's gifting us with what we would never have been able to purchase on our own was timely affirming of God's presence with us."
—*"Pastor Roz," Rev. Dr. Rosalyn Nichols, Freedom's Chapel Christian Church*

Table of Contents

Acknowledgments — xi
Preface — xiii

Part One: The Early Years — 1
My 'First Life' — 3
Living in Hurley — 9
Accepted on Probation — 13
Korean War, Air Force Changed My Plans — 15
Amarillo Air Force Base — 19
Next Assignment: Newfoundland — 23
Discharged and Back to Civilian Life — 33

Part Two: Hollywood Years — 35
NBC Page and Famous Actors — 37
Finally, a Film and a Wife — 45
VA Calling — 47

Part Three: Montessori Education and Lab School — 55
Learning About Montessori Education — 57
My Own Montessori School — 63
Surprise Visitor Leads to Career Change — 65
Back to New Mexico — 67

Part Four: Dr. Canady, Professor — 71
From Lab School in Silver City to a University — 73
From Tucson to Tuscaloosa — 77
Learning to Fly in Tahlequah — 85

Part Five: Pilot Meets God on 5,000-Foot Runway — 89
The Flying Event That Changed My Life — 91

Part Six: Stained-Glass Ministry — 95
The Pilot Becomes an Artist Again — 97
New Position for Shirley, Artist Calling for Bob — 111
Stained-Glass Ministry Partnership — 114
From Lexington to Memphis — 117
Cairo Baptist Church Stained Glass — 125
Respect, Honesty, and Race — 129
First United Methodist Church — 138
The Artist and My Right Brain — 143
About the Author — 151

Dedication

To my beloved, Shirley, my inspiration and collaborator on this and other creative endeavors.

Acknowledgments

Photographers:

Mark Stansbury, executive assistant for community relations, leadership staff for the University of Memphis president, Shirley Raines; Shelby Raines, photographer of Cairo Baptist Church's stained-glass windows.

Pastors and church leaders:

Some church pastors and leaders have moved to other churches, retired, or are deceased. While many people in the congregations worked with me, I have listed the pastors and church leaders who communicated most closely with me during the creation and installation of the stained-glass windows. Please forgive any omissions.

Trinity Hill United Methodist Church, Rev. Don Dilday and Bill Ashbrook, Lexington, Kentucky; St. Paul's United Methodist Church, Rev. Marcia Woodyard, Frankfort, Kentucky; Wesley Center, University of Memphis; Greater Wright's Chapel African Methodist Episcopal Church, Rev. Walter Cox (deceased), Arlington, Tennessee; Canaan Baptist Church, Brother Paul Adams and Freddie Graves (deceased), Ashland, Mississippi; Greater Payne Chapel African Methodist Episcopal Church, Rev. Quinten L. Smith, Memphis, Tennessee; Friendship United Methodist Church, Pastor Cynthia Davis with Addie Nunnerly, Millington, Tennessee; First United Methodist Church, Rev. Martha Wagley, Memphis, Tennessee; Freedom's Chapel Christian Church, Dr. Rosalyn R. Nichols, Memphis, Tennessee; Philippians V Multi-Ministry Center, Pastor Shirley Prince, Memphis, Tennessee; St. John's Missionary Baptist Church, Rev. Keith McGhee, Drummonds, Tennessee; and Old and New Rebuilt Cairo Baptist Church, member Carey Raines, Alamo, Tennessee.

Acknowledgments

Children:
Lynnette Canady, Scott Canady, Larkellen Canady, and stepson Brian Scott Smith.

Grandchildren:
Christina Mills, Damien Roberts, Michelle Harvey, and Riley and Bryson Smith.

Great-grandchildren:
Kathryn Mills; Garvin, Addam, and Tristan Harvey; and Nairobi and Eleanor Roberts.

Other family members:
Mitchell Mills, Kevin Harvey, AssereTH Zapata de Roberts, and Marti Overton.

Memoriam:
Parents and family: Pauline and Bob Canady; Jake, Ray, and Betty Canady.
Academics: Dr. Van Allen, University of Arizona; Dr. Virginia Purcell and Netter Worthington, Chapman College; and Mildred Carr, acting coach.

Special appreciation to Jacque Hillman, the editor of *Life Stories: Educator, Painter, Pilot, Stained-Glass Artist*, and her team. She is senior editor/CEO of The HillHelen Group, LLC, Mesa, Arizona.

Preface

The idea for this book originated many years ago on the balcony of a penthouse overlooking the Mississippi River. My wife, Dr. Shirley Raines, had just been appointed as the president of the University of Memphis and was the first woman to hold that office. We were attending a reception at the house of a prominent supporter of the university.

From attending many of these events, I learned to speak to the host and each of the people there, then find myself a quiet corner and sip my glass of wine. The balcony seemed to be the ideal spot. As I enjoyed the magnificent view of the Mississippi River and the *M* bridge, I discovered a man on the other side of the balcony. He came over with a sheepish grin and said, "I see you've discovered my hiding place." We both had a good laugh and began a conversation that lasted the rest of the evening.

I soon realized that the reason I was doing most of the talking was because he was an author and was gathering ideas for a book. By the time the party ended, I had told him most of the unusual events of my life. He gave me his name and telephone number and told me to call him if I was interested in writing a book with him. He said, "I see these various events as 'chapters.'"

Since that night on the balcony, I have told my unusual stories many times to various groups of people and to the congregations of fifteen churches. My talks have invariably ended with someone saying, "You should write a book."

Part One

The Early Years

From the Canady Photo Collection

Two-year-old Bob Canady and his four-year-old sister, Betty, eventually moved to Hurley, New Mexico, with their parents.

From the Canady Photo Collection

Houses line Bungalow Street in Hurley, New Mexico, where Bob Canady spent most of his childhood.

1
My 'First Life'

My story began in a small farmhouse near the town of Damascus, Arkansas, where I was born during the Great Depression. It was not a good time for my family to gain another mouth to feed. I had two older brothers and a sister, and my father had just learned that the bank where he kept his money had closed. His money was gone.

My birth not only happened at a difficult time, but it was almost the beginning and end for me. I was born with a thin membrane covering my face. One of the women present quickly removed the membrane, just as the doctor finally arrived. He told her that she probably saved my life because it was impossible for me to breathe. Later, when things settled down, another woman said, "You know that the veil means he is going to be artistic." At that time, artistic or not, I was another mouth to feed.

My father had started out as a sharecropper and managed to save enough money to buy the small farm where he worked. He had no formal education, and owning that farm was the most important thing in his life. Suddenly, my mother and father found themselves with four children and no money or place to live as they could not pay the mortgage for the farm. They had no choice but to sell what little of value they owned, load up an old car, a Model T pickup, and join the thousands of other people heading west.

The sudden change from dreams of owning their own farm to concerns about survival left my mother and father with a bitterness that always stayed with them. They believed that not only had the government let them down but even God had abandoned them, a feeling they had for the rest of their lives.

> "The influence of a mother upon the lives of her children cannot be measured. They know and absorb her example and attitudes when it comes to questions of honesty, temperance, kindness, and industry."
> —Billy Graham

Rumors of work available in the fields of Texas and California kept them slowly moving west, but they were running out of money for food and gasoline. They made it to a rest stop in southern New Mexico and realized they could go no farther. The rest stop was full of people just like themselves.

My father saw two large trucks coming on the highway, and he went out to the road and flagged them down, standing in the middle of the road to stop them. The drivers were working on the highway a few miles from the rest stop. Dad told them that he would work with them all day for some food and gasoline. They agreed, and that evening, we were back on the road, heading to a town called Hurley, New Mexico, where the men told my father there was a copper mine that was going to reopen soon.

We made it to Hurley, where we learned that the copper mill and smelter would be opening in a few months and there would be a job for my father. He was told that a small house one mile north of town was empty and he could use it. The men also told my father about a gold mine in the mountains where they needed a carpenter.

The "house" we were free to use turned out to be a rusty, tin shack with two small rooms, one bed with no mattress, one table, and a couple of chairs. There was no electricity or running water, and the door was missing on the outhouse. Fortunately, there was a good well with clean water. A small gas station nearby sold basic groceries, and my father convinced the owner that when he got paid from his job at the gold mine, he would pay for what his family charged.

My father got everyone settled the best he could and then got into the Model T pickup and headed for the gold mine. Before he arrived at the mine, Dad had taken all the tools that a carpenter would use and put them in the back of the old pickup. When the foreman at the mine saw the tools, he immediately hired my father, and Dad worked as a carpenter at the gold mine until the copper mine opened.

> "Necessity is the mother of taking chances."
> —Mark Twain

This painting by Polly Canady, Dr. Canady's mother, shows Superstition Mountains. She was self-taught. She also looked at photos of clothes in magazines and created clothes for her children and grandchildren.
From the Canady Photo Collection

Photo courtesy of Old Hurley Store Museum

The Old Hurley Store, at 99 Cortez Avenue in Hurley, New Mexico, is now an antique store and includes a model railroad. The property, which is owned by Becky and Don Spann, has more than 20,000 square feet of store, loft, apartment, and warehouse space.

From the Canady Photo Collection

This postcard shows a landscape view of Hurley, New Mexico.

From the Canady Photo Collection

Bob Canady was fourteen or fifteen in this Hurley High School photo. His mother made his jacket and shirt.

2
Living in Hurley

Hurley, a company town, consisted of row after row of identical houses. I was only three years old when we moved into one of the houses in Hurley, but I still remember going into the house for the first time. It had a front porch, living room, dining room, kitchen, back porch, two bedrooms, and a real bathroom. I lived in that house with my mother, father, two brothers, and sister until I graduated from high school.

Living in a company town was a unique experience. After what our family and many of the other families had been through, it offered a feeling of security. Even though much of the work was done in rotating shifts, most jobs were easy and paid well. The company covered all maintenance of the town as well as medical expenses, and it also controlled the schools.

One of the negative aspects of company-led schools is that many decisions were made by people with little or no experience. Some teachers were hired because they could not get a job anywhere else. In those early years, a high school diploma was the students' primary goal because it was required for employment by the company. As the mine, the mill, and the smelter grew, more workers were hired, and a high school diploma was required. All students who showed up for class earned a diploma.

Unfortunately, I was a victim of the poor education system in Hurley. There was no kindergarten at that time, so children started in first grade when they were six years old. One year when school was to begin, the first-grade teacher didn't have enough children to fill her class, so she came to the homes of children who were five years old and asked if their mothers would let their children start school early.

> "The more that you read, the more things you will know; the more that you learn, the more places you'll go."
> —Dr. Seuss

When the teacher came to our house, my mother told her that I had just turned five and she didn't think I was ready for school. The teacher asked me if I knew my ABCs, and I quickly rattled off the alphabet, which my sister, Betty, had taught me.

The teacher clapped her hands and said, "That's wonderful!" My mother was still opposed to me starting school, but I begged her to let me try. She reluctantly agreed to let me go—a decision she later regretted.

I went from first grade through eighth grade, always behind the rest of the class. No student ever failed because the teachers believed that if they failed a student, it would reflect poorly on the teacher. But when the junior high principal saw my test scores at the end of eighth grade, he said I should repeat eighth grade because I would never make it in high school.

He came to talk to my mother to see if she would convince me that I should repeat eighth grade. He didn't know what he was getting into. My mother pointed her finger in his face and said, "Oh, no—I said he wasn't ready to go to school, but you people thought you knew better than me. Now, if he isn't ready for high school, you tell him, not me!"

I went to high school and struggled with every class, as predicted, but I played football and basketball, and in that school, you did not fail athletes. At the end of my junior year, the counselor told me to take a lot of shop courses during my senior year because I would never be accepted into college. She didn't know the power of sports.

"Children must be taught how to think, not what to think."
—Margaret Mead

From the Canady Photo Collection

Dr. Canady's father worked at the Chino Copper Mine in Hurley, New Mexico. Kennecott Copper Corporation operated the Chino Mine.

From the Canady Photo Collection

Bob Canady, above left, worked as a summer cowhand at Gilchrist Ranch. He was a junior or senior in high school when this photo was taken with another summer cowhand.

3
Accepted on Probation

I was accepted into college on a probationary basis because of a football scholarship and was warned that I had to maintain a C average to keep the scholarship. The dean was aware of my pathetic transcript, so when he learned about my talent in art, he suggested that I take some art classes to help keep up my grade average. He also was an avid football fan.

I had always been interested in art, but my artistic expression was usually confined to cartooning. When I was four years old, my older brothers, Jake and Ray, took me with them to school once. The teacher sat me at a desk and gave me a piece of paper and some crayons. When I finished my picture, I held it up and the teacher asked me what it was. I told him it was a dog. He said the dog didn't have a tail. I said, "It's a streamlined dog." The whole class broke up laughing, and I knew that I was onto something.

> "Painting is just another way of keeping a diary."
> —Pablo Picasso

As it turned out, the head of the art department loved cartoons, and I soon found that the As I received in my three art classes would ensure that I could keep my C average and my scholarship. I became the first art major on a football scholarship in the school's history.

From the Canady Photo Collection

Bob attended Western New Mexico University on a football scholarship.

4
Korean War, Air Force Changed My Plans

During the summer, those of us whose fathers worked for the Kennecott Mining Company in Hurley were given jobs, which was necessary to pay for college expenses. One summer during the Korean War, a buddy of mine got drafted. I realized I could be next. The thought of being in the infantry on a Korean battlefield caused me to think of some alternatives. I decided to join the Navy since my older brothers had been in the Navy in World War II.

I went to the nearest recruiter, who was in El Paso, Texas, and told him I wanted to join the Navy. He said they were not taking any more recruits at that time. He saw I was disappointed and said, "There's an Air Force recruiter across the street. Check with him."

Half an hour later, I had signed paperwork for four years of duty in the Air Force. All I needed was to show my birth certificate.

I called the records office in Little Rock, Arkansas, and they assured me that my birth certificate would arrive in a couple of days. A birth certificate arrived a week later, and I was on my way to El Paso and the US Air Force. There was just one problem. The birth certificate wasn't mine. Some of the information was correct and some of it was not. I showed it to the recruiter, and he said, "The Air Force says I must see a birth certificate—this is a birth certificate. Welcome to the United States Air Force."

When I got on the train to go to Lackland Air Force Base, where I was to report for duty, I recognized a guy I had known at the university. We sat together and tried to figure out what the Air Force would be like. We had been told that, during boot camp, we would be given an opportunity to choose the kind of work we wanted in the Air Force.

> "Word to the Nation: Guard zealously your right to serve in the armed forces, for without them, there will be no other rights to guard."
> —President John F. Kennedy

When we arrived at the air base, we looked out the window and saw two air policemen on the platform who were directing the recruits to a bus. They were wearing blue uniforms with white lanyards that went over their shoulders and were hooked onto big, shiny .45 pistols. Their caps had a white cover on top and their black boots were covered with white spats.

I looked at my buddy, and he looked at me. We agreed that we wanted to be air policemen. We both put that down as our preference. By the time we finished basic training, we learned that the air police was the least desirable job in the Air Force, but it was too late to change our minds.

From the Canady Photo Collection

After Bob went through basic training at Lackland Air Force Base, he played wide receiver at Amarillo Air Force Base for the base football team, the Jets.

From the Canady Photo Collection

This later photo of the Amarillo Air Force Base Exchange shows the popular cars of the servicemen and women. The airmen could pick up some Coca-Colas, cigarettes, antacids, and candies. Gas was twenty-five cents per gallon back then.

5
Amarillo Air Force Base

We were sent from Lackland Air Force Base in Texas to Georgia for air police training. After completing training, I was sent to the Amarillo Air Force Base in Texas. The air base had been reopened after serving as an important base for World War II fighters and bombers.

The citizens of Amarillo had mixed feelings about having hundreds of young men on their streets and in their bars. As air police, we were told we had been carefully picked to handle the situation. I looked sharp in my dress uniform and was assigned to the main gate on the base and to the air policemen who were on town patrol. The Amarillo city police and the county police were so glad to have me that they gave me a special desk in the county police station in the center of town.

The first encounter between our airmen and the high school boys came as expected in a high school parking lot. The air policeman assigned to the area gave up, and I went with a deputy to restore order. Later, I went to the high school and apologized to the principal. He assured me that the high school boys would be reprimanded, and I assured him that the whole high school area would be off-limits to our men.

We all knew that this encounter was only the beginning and more had to be done to entertain the men. A former football coach was found and transferred to our base.

Headquarters' public affairs office announced that we were going to have a base football team. Excitement spread immediately, and I was one of the first to get my name on the list for tryouts.

> "Off we go into the wild blue yonder.... Basic flying rules: Try to stay in the middle of the air. Do not go near the edges of it. The edges of the air can be recognized by the appearance of ground, buildings, sea, trees, and interstellar space. It is much more difficult to fly there."
> —Air Force saying

Tryouts were held on a dirt field on one corner of the base, and a strange-looking group of guys showed up, mostly wearing fatigues and sweatshirts with the logos of impressive teams for which they had played.

I knew a player who was a star quarterback at his college, so when the coach asked what position we played, I said, "End," and quickly added, "Wide receiver," which was the latest fad in football.

The coach soon learned I wasn't the fastest player on the field, but I followed and executed plays well as a receiver. I convinced him I could play on the defense, too. I became the starting offensive and defensive end for the Amarillo Air Force Base Jets.

When we got to the flight line and prepared to board before our first away game, we were issued parachutes, which were required on all military airplanes. After the parachutes were strapped onto us and we were about to board, one of our huge linemen, who played tackle, looked down at the parachute and then looked at the airplane. He was not about to board. He had been bragging and acting the part of a war hero who planned to save the country until he saw those parachutes. He looked down at the parachute harness and ran to the nearest bathroom to throw up. At the end of the line, he reluctantly boarded the small C-47 airplane, strapped himself in, and closed his eyes. When we landed at Randolph Air Force Base, he was ready to do battle with a talented group of former football greats from impressive universities. We lost the game by a score of 49-7.

When we boarded the plane to return to Amarillo Air Force Base, we felt good about surviving our first game. I was pleased with catching a pass for our only touchdown. But I also received a shoulder injury from attempting to block a large offensive tackle.

We ended the season having a great time as a team and won the rest of our games. The biggest thrill of that experience happened when my oldest brother, Jake, who was teaching in Tucumcari, New Mexico, across the state line from Amarillo, came to one game. At a home game in Amarillo, he was given a cot in the players' dormitory next to my room. He even sampled the excellent food the players were served in the dining room.

After football season ended, I continued as an air policeman. On one occasion, I went to sleep late and woke early to big news: A very important visitor was coming, and I was in charge of the detail. I told the messenger I had been up all night policing downtown and to get someone else.

Then I asked, "Who is this important person?" President Dwight D. Eisenhower was the answer. I said, "I'll be ready in five minutes."

President Eisenhower was coming to Amarillo to meet with local citizens and farmers to assure them that economic help was coming. He also emphasized that they were important to the Air Force for their support of the base as part of the war effort.

When Air Force One taxied up to the area I was assigned, I stationed myself at the point where President Eisenhower would be leaving the airport to go downtown and meet with dignitaries and locals. When his open convertible came by me, I saluted the president by snapping to attention and holding my M1 rifle in a salute position. He returned the salute and said, "Good job, Sergeant." I wasn't really called a sergeant in the Air Force—I was an airman first class—but if he said I was a sergeant, I was a sergeant.

Photo courtesy of firstairforceone.org

This Columbine II is also known as Air Force One. The first Air Force One, which landed at Amarillo Air Force Base, brought President Eisenhower to talk to local government officials. Eisenhower spoke to a young military policeman named Bob Canady.

6
Next Assignment: Newfoundland

At Amarillo, I spent time involved in things other than police work and playing football. I served on honor guards, played football for two seasons for a base team, and drew cartoons for the base newspaper.

Most servicemen want to spend part of their experience overseas. When overseas openings were available, they were listed on the main office bulletin board. Airmen could indicate that they wanted to go to one of the overseas bases. The problem was they couldn't choose a particular one. The next listed locations were Germany (3), Japan (2), and Newfoundland (1).

I had always wanted to go to Germany, and the odds were in my favor. A few days later, the captain called me into his office and said, "Congratulations, you'll love Newfoundland." My disappointment didn't last long. I was looking for a new experience, and I had a feeling that this was certainly going to be unique.

After a five-day leave with my family in Hurley, I took a long train ride to New Brunswick, New Jersey, where I was put on a bus to the Brooklyn Naval Yard with twenty other "lucky" airmen going to Newfoundland.

The bus ride into New York City was an incredible experience for someone who lived much of his life in southern New Mexico, but the real thrill was passing under the Statue of Liberty on our way out to sea.

When we entered the deep water, the small ship we were on moved up and down with each wave. Most of the airmen put their hands over their mouths and ran for the head downstairs. Some of them didn't make it.

Fortunately, I have never been bothered with motion sickness, and I stayed on the bow of the ship, enjoying the dolphins who seemed to be playing with us.

That night, the rocking of the ship caused me to sleep so soundly that I was surprised when someone woke me up and it was morning. Everyone seemed to be excited about something. When I came on deck, I discovered the reason. We were tied to the pier in St. Johns Harbor, Newfoundland.

The harbor is surrounded by beautiful, high, sloping hills on all sides. Small, colorful houses are scattered up and down the hills, and boats of all kinds are anchored or tied near the shore.

We were told that we were free to explore St. Johns, but the ship would be leaving for Stephenville, which is on the western shore of Newfoundland. We were to be back at precisely eighteen hundred hours. "Don't miss the boat," we were warned. "It is a long walk to Stephenville."

Stephenville, Newfoundland, is a small town next to Ernest Harmon Air Force Base, our destination. The base was in a beautiful location with pine trees on three sides and a rocky shoreline on the ocean side.

Security on the base was not a major concern, and air policemen were there primarily for show. They manned the entrance to the base, patrolled the fuel tanks that were on the edge of the base, and broke up fights that were caused by homesick airmen who had too much to drink.

I soon learned that the primary problem at Ernest Harmon was low morale. The residents of Stephenville were wonderful, but the town was small and the kind of entertainment the airmen wanted was nonexistent. An exciting evening in Stephenville was a potluck dinner at the church.

Shortly after arriving at the base, I was promoted, which meant that I spent less time on guard duty and patrol and more time in the office. To entertain myself, I did what I had always done; I started drawing cartoons.

There are few environments in the world where you will find more materials for jokes and cartoons than in the military. I believe my first cartoon was about the first sergeant insisting on the men policing the area around the barracks during a snowstorm. I showed some of the men waist-deep in snow, proudly holding up a piece of paper they had found, while others only had their legs sticking out as they searched under the snow. The cartoon was placed on the bulletin board, and even the first sergeant got a kick out of it.

It wasn't long before the men started looking for the next cartoon and complaining when it wasn't there. I was surprised to find out that copies were made and distributed throughout the base.

The officer in charge of the PX, better known as the beer hall, wanted a couple of cartoons to hang up. A standing joke on the base was about the low-alcohol beer that was served in the PX. The airmen knew they had to get to the PX as soon as it opened at six and drink continually until ten, when it closed, before they could get a buzz on.

The problem this caused was frequent trips to the head. In one cartoon, I showed four men drinking beer at the table they had moved into the head. Soon, my cartoons were showing up on bulletin boards all over the base.

The air police worked closely with the Royal Canadian Mounted Police in Stephenville. One of the Mounties asked me to draw a cartoon for their office. I told him I would be glad to, but I didn't want to offend anyone. He assured me that I wasn't likely to cause offense and that everyone, including the townspeople, had a wonderful sense of humor.

I had asked a Mountie earlier how drivers knew who was supposed to stop since there were no stop signs at the intersections in town. "Oh, that's easy," he said. "If one car honks his horn first, the other has to stop."

In my cartoon, I drew two cars crashed together at an intersection. One of the drivers was holding his hands out, explaining to the Mountie, "I 'onked me bloomin' 'orn and 'e 'it me anyway!" Understand that most of the residents of Stephenville did not pronounce the beginning *H* sound when they spoke.

> "Ninety-eight percent of Canadians say, 'Oh chit!' before going into the ditch on a slippery road. The other 2 percent are from Newfoundland, and they say, 'Hold my beer and watch this.' "
> —Anonymous

Early one morning, the desk sergeant came to my room and told me that the base commander wanted to talk to me. I took off my fatigues, put on my blue uniform, and hurried to headquarters. I felt like a kid going to the principal's office, wondering what I had done wrong.

The commander was a young lieutenant colonel, highly respected for his strict supervision of the base. I entered his office, stood at attention, and announced myself in a military manner.

He gave me a stern look and said, "Are you the one who is responsible for the cartoons on 'my' bulletin boards?"

"Yes, sir," I managed to say.

"Well, I put important information on those boards, and all the men see are your cartoons." Then he smiled and said, "What do you think we should do about it?"

I just shrugged, and then he came around his desk, pointed to two comfortable chairs, and said, "Sit down and listen to my idea." We sat down in the chairs, and I soon learned that my life in the Air Force was about to make a dramatic change.

The commander told me that one of the reasons he was sent to the base was to tighten some of the regulations regarding wasted materials and wasted man-hours. He said that posters and even threats that appeared around the base were having little impact on the problem. "All they seem to notice on the bulletin boards is one of your cartoons, so why don't we use them to get my message across?"

The impact of what he was saying was so strong that I was speechless, so he continued with his idea. "We could have you create a character to appear on each message, which would be illustrated in a cartoon."

"Like a little Scottish character in a kilt," I added.

"That's the idea," he said.

And, I quickly added, "We could have a contest to name the character and the winner gets a three-day pass to Corner Brook." The commander hesitated for a moment and then agreed that it was a good idea.

The commander got up, and I assumed the meeting was over, but he indicated that I should follow him. We went down the hall and entered a room with four large drafting tables. At two of the tables, draftsmen were busy at work on some complicated-looking diagrams.

I still get a chill when I remember what the commander said. He introduced me to the two men at their drafting tables and then pointed to an empty table and told the men, "This will be Canady's table, so give him whatever supplies he needs." Then he looked at me and said, "You will be transferred to the Headquarters Squadron and work directly with the first sergeant and me. You will be expected to be here from eight to five. I will inform the first sergeant of our project and he will assist you with planning the details."

The first sergeant was excited about the project and had some excellent ideas for the promotion of the plan, which he officially titled the "Cost-Conscious Program, Ernest Harmon."

I created a little Scottish character, wearing a kilt, vest, buckle shoes, long plaid socks, and a tam on his head. The contest for naming him was a big success. The little guy became "Thrifty McNifty." The posters were instantly popular, and the little character started showing up all over the base. The base commander expressed his appreciation by placing a wonderful letter of commendation in my official records.

As I stated earlier, the military provides constant materials for a cartoonist. To prove that point, the base commander and three other officers decided to go on a moose hunt north of the base. And they got lost! The air and sea rescue helicopter was dispatched and finally found them. The whole base was enjoying a good laugh, especially the enlisted men.

The day after the officers returned, the base commander came by my drawing desk and said, "Well, Canady, I suppose you will make a big thing of this with your cartoons."

"Oh, no!" I replied. "I wouldn't do that, sir."

"Well, you should," he said. "Come into my office; I have an idea. How about this? We will make a little booklet of cartoons about the moose hunt and sell them on the base for one dollar apiece. They should sell like hotcakes. Then we will donate the money to the town of Stephenville."

My admiration for this unusual man went to a new level.

The booklet was created, and the sales were as expected. Just how many booklets sold, I will never know because another miraculous event in my life was about to happen.

I had lunch one day with the first sergeant. He knew I was getting near the end of my four-year tour in the Air Force. He told me that because the Korean War was over, the military was beginning to reduce in number and, as an incentive, those who planned to return to college could be discharged six months early. He said, "According to your records, you only have six months left, so if we can get a verification from your college that you will enroll, you could get discharged now."

Before I could thoroughly process this information, the sergeant added, "I am also ready to be discharged and will be driving my car back to the States in two weeks. You could come with me if we can get the verification from the dean of your college."

I told him that it was a small college in New Mexico, and I couldn't imagine getting verification that soon. He assured me that he had the ability to communicate with anyone in the world. All he needed was the name of the college and the dean's name.

The next day when I came to work, I found a note on my drawing board telling me to go to the first sergeant's office. When I entered his office, he told me to go to a phone at a nearby desk. He then picked up his phone and punched in a series of numbers.

A few minutes later, he told me to pick up the other phone. My college dean said, "Hello, Bob. I hear you will be back with us soon."

A few days later, I was on a ferry with the sergeant and his car on our way to Nova Scotia and New England. The sergeant drove me most of the way to LaGuardia Airport in New York, where I boarded an American Airlines Constellation bound for El Paso, Texas. It was a short bus ride from El Paso to my home in Hurley, where I spent a few days before driving my little Plymouth Business Coupe back to El Paso to receive my discharge from the Air Force.

Ernest Harmon Air Force Base

During the early part of World War II, the Germans' fleet of U-boats was terrorizing convoy and support ships in the North Atlantic. Britain was losing the Battle of the Atlantic and needed more warships. The United States worried that if England was overthrown, Hitler's army would invade North America. This led to the 'Destroyers for Base Agreement,' signed on September 2, 1940. For fifty destroyer warships, the United States would get ninety-nine-year leases to build military bases on Newfoundland, then owned by Britain.

Photos from the Canady Photo Collection

Ernest Harmon Air Force Base would ensure protection of North America and act as a refueling station for planes and convoys traveling across the Atlantic Ocean. Visit hiddennewfoundland.ca/harmon-air-force-base for details.

Ernest Harmon Air Force Base

After the war, the airfield continued to be used as a refueling point, and on June 23, 1948, the base was renamed the Ernest Harmon Air Force Base in honor of Captain Ernest Emery Harmon, an Army Air Corps pilot who was killed in an air crash in 1933. The deepwater port nearby was also given the name Port Harmon at this time. Stephenville International Airport uses a portion of the original air field, which was closed in 1966.

Photos from the Canady Photo Collection

From the Canady Photo Collection

This two-door, hardtop, red and white 1955 Plymouth Belvedere was Bob Canady's dream car.

7
Discharged and Back to Civilian Life

The day after I returned home, I received a call from the company power plant's supervisor, who wanted to talk to me. I met him at his home, and he told me about a company policy that had recently been announced. To honor men who had been employed at the company when they entered the armed forces, the time they had spent in the service could be applied to their seniority if the company rehired them. In other words, he would give me a job in the power plant that required at least four years of seniority.

Work in the power plant was clean, easy, and paid well. The problem was that it was shift work, and I wouldn't be able to go to college.

"No problem," the supervisor said. "I can put you on the evening shift full time."

I left his house feeling a little guilty for being rewarded for "service for my country," which had been so enjoyable.

The next day, on my way to meet with the dean and register for college, I passed by a car dealership that had a beautiful, new 1955 Plymouth Belvedere slowly rotating on a circular platform. I pulled over to the curb, parked, and just stared at it. It was a two-door hardtop, painted red and white, and had a V8 engine. I reluctantly drove away to make sure I wouldn't be late for the meeting with the dean.

The dean came around his desk and shook my hand. He was obviously pleased to have another Canady on the college football team. My two older brothers had been standouts on the team a few years earlier.

> "Hollywood's like a warehouse. It's just a place that you go. What's interesting in the warehouse has to do with the creative people."
> —Val Kilmer

I told him about my job at the company power plant and that I would be enrolling as a full-time day student. "But you won't be playing football," he said with a frown.

"No," I thought. "But I will be driving that red and white Plymouth with the white sidewall tires."

Along with my required courses, I took some art courses and a drama course. It was then that I discovered that I had a talent for acting. After I had the lead in a one-act play, the drama teacher said, "You know, Bob, if I was young, good-looking, and talented, I would go out to Hollywood and give it a try." And then he added, "Especially if I had the GI Bill to pay for acting lessons."

I realized he was serious. I shook my head and said, "I don't know anyone out there."

He smiled and said, "But I do."

It was the end of the semester. I had always wanted to see California and I had some time off, so, I decided, why not go?

My drama teacher gave me the name and address of a well-known drama coach who was also an agent. I couldn't use the GI Bill, but she made a call, and I was hired as a page at the NBC Studio in Hollywood. It was an exciting time for NBC because the new NBC "color" studio was about to open in Burbank.

Part Two

Hollywood Years

From the Canady Photo Collection

Bob was hired as a page at the NBC Studio in Burbank, California.

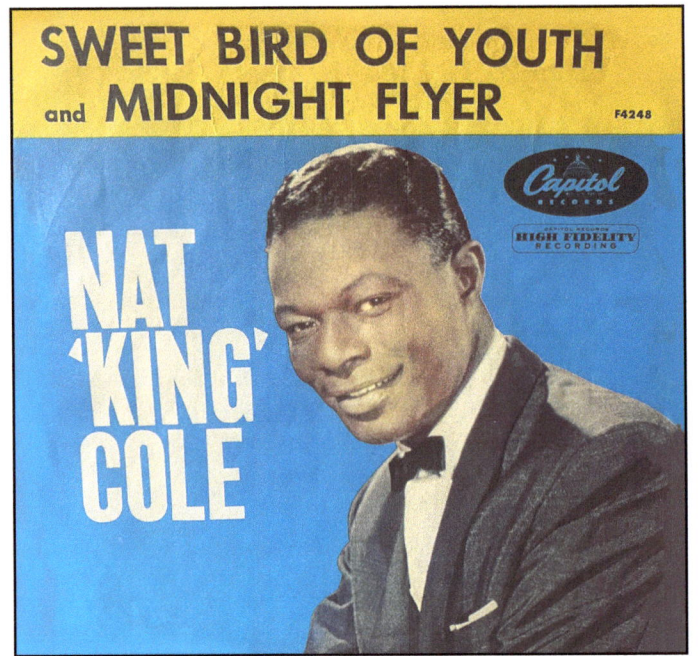 

From the Canady Photo Collection

Above left: Bob Canady thanked Nat King Cole for making 'my teenage dates so successful when we danced to his recording of 'Star Dust.' ' Above right: Canady also recalled when Bob Hope tripped coming out of the hallway phone booth and joked, 'Got to get those roller skates oiled.'

8
NBC Page and Famous Actors

Since I was one of the few full-time pages, I was put in charge of the artists' entrance of the new studio. I was given a list of personnel who were allowed in the building and later actors who would be entering and the dressing rooms they were to use. I had no trouble recognizing the regular workers, the staff, and the actors, but the stars without their makeup in the morning were sometimes difficult to recognize.

The performers entered from the parking lot though a special door near my desk to get the keys to their dressing rooms and to check for messages left for them. One morning, I was told to go to the parking lot and escort world-famous singers Nelson Eddy and Jeanette MacDonald, who arrived in a Rolls Royce limousine. They had been more successful in bringing classical music into the average home and even to teenagers than anyone else at that time. I remember watching Nelson in a Mountie uniform singing to Jeanette in a Canadian snow scene. I knew I was seeing a world-class performance.

Part of my responsibility was to periodically check on the other pages who were stationed in various studios and rehearsal rooms throughout the building. This gave me a rare chance to watch actors going over their lines for a live show. I also saw singers going over the music with their pianists. I enjoyed an experience few other people had.

I knew Nat King Cole was rehearsing in a particular private room with a famous music director, Nelson Riddle. I entered the room quietly and found a chair in the corner. Nat King Cole motioned to a closer chair and said, "Come on over and watch this man make me look good." I had heard what a great singer he was and how humble Mr. Cole was. Now I believed it.

> "I'm not playing for other musicians. We're trying to reach the guy who works all day and wants to spend a buck at night. We'll keep him happy."
> —Nat King Cole

During his break, he asked me if I was a singer and I told him, "Only in my dreams," but I had to thank him for making my teenage dates so successful when we danced to his recording of "Star Dust." He pointed to Nelson Riddle and said, "See there, what you did?"

Mr. Cole found out I was a struggling actor and said, "Hang in there and don't give up." He referred to sad times when he felt like giving up. He was performing in famous hotels to sold-out audiences, but they wouldn't let him stay in the hotels where he performed.

As the senior page, I was able to choose my assignments for the live one-hour shows that were broadcast weekly from different studios. I chose the one every page wanted, the Lux Studio Theater, starring Gordon MacRae. He was my favorite of all the entertainers and other famous people I encountered.

I will always cherish the moments I shared with Gordon and his beautiful and talented wife, Sheila MacRae. Each studio had an observation booth with a one-way window, which gave the people off the set a full view and sound to hear the actors, as well as the direction to the camera people and sound systems. We could see the actors, but they could not see us. What a wonderful experience for a would-be actor.

My most amazing experiences in that setting were my conversations with Sheila MacRae. She loved talking about Gordon and his unique talents as an actor and singer.

Our favorite story was about a time when Gordon found that a singer whom he knew well could not fulfill his commitment to sing at a presidential fundraiser because he was sick. Gordon immediately called the chairman of the committee and said he could come and fill in for the singer. That was Gordon!

I went with him to the event after quickly helping him change clothes and gather the music he planned to sing. We arrived just as the announcer was about to announce that the singer would not be able to perform. The announcer quickly substituted, "Ladies and gentlemen, we have a surprise for you. Please welcome to the stage Mr. Gordon MacRae!"

Gordon then took the music to the piano player. When we heard the first notes, we knew the pianist was playing the song in the wrong key. Gordon took a deep breath and gave a perfect performance that drew thunderous applause.

It would be impossible to pick the most memorable event that I experienced during my time as a page at the NBC Studio, but the following event would be near the top. Bob Hope was scheduled to rehearse his Alaska Christmas show in one of the large rehearsal studios. I looked forward to seeing him in person for the first time.

Ginger Rogers, who was to be on the show, came in the door first and told me to tell Mr. Hope that she was out in the parking lot having breakfast at the breakfast bar. When Bob Hope arrived, I relayed the message to him. He simply said, "Tell Miss Rogers that I hope she has a nice breakfast."

Later in the morning, Mr. Hope came out to my desk and asked if there was a public telephone around. I showed him the booth across the hall, and he made his call. When he came out of the booth, he tripped and almost fell to the floor. My heart jumped in my throat, but he managed to get his footing. As he started down the hall to the studio, he looked over his shoulder at me and quipped, "Got to get those roller skates oiled." For most of my life, I have believed that I am the only person in the world to have Bob Hope deliver a joke to an audience of one!

As I was able to choose the shows where I wanted to work, I also selected the Tennessee Ernie Ford show, which led to one of the most exciting moments of my life.

Ralph Edwards hosted the "This Is Your Life" program across the hall in another studio. When he was going to visit Tennessee Ernie Ford as the star who was going to be surprised, I was a part of the event. When Ralph came into the studio, Ernie turned around and looked at me just as Ralph was saying, "Tennessee Ernie Ford, this is your life."

> "An actor is at most a poet and at least an entertainer."
> —Marlon Brando

Ernie put his hands on his cheeks and said, "My God, I must look like a sack of onions."

My days as an NBC page were filled with meeting special stars, jokes, and surprises, but I must write about a nightmarish event that happened soon after the new NBC building was completed and was receiving large crowds to watch the live shows as they were being seen in homes all around the world.

My job became more difficult. The large crowds were loud and hard to control. Then the "nightmare" began. The latest rock star was Tommy Sands, and he was having his television debut at the new NBC Studio. We expected to have a huge crowd, and when everyone arrived, they were almost impossible to control.

Then, to add to the control problem, an NBC official came out to the front and informed me that the local newspaper had printed that Elvis Presley was going to be there to support his friend Tommy Sands. The plan was to sneak Elvis into the building through a private door and hide him upstairs in the control booth.

I looked at the control room booth and there was someone sitting in a chair with a hat and sunglasses. I went back to the crowd and said, "There is someone in the control booth with sunglasses, but it is definitely not Elvis." One young lady was crying because she was going home without an autograph, so I took her little book and signed, "Bob Canady, NBC page."

Sorry, but Elvis has left the building.

We will never know whether Elvis was there, but if he was, it was nice of him to thank me for keeping his secret. By the way, Tommy Sands was wonderful, but he was never Elvis Presley.

Each week, the list of famous people grew larger. You can imagine what a thrill it was for an ex-Golden Gloves boxer to shake hands with the world heavyweight champion Jack Dempsey.

I will not attempt to list all the famous performers and newsmakers who came to the NBC Studio, but I want to share some special moments with you.

One morning, I sat just out of camera range during a live broadcast of a soap opera-type play. In the scene, I watched a well-known actor who was playing the role of a father visiting his daughter. He was in the bedroom getting dressed for dinner. Well, he was supposed to be in the bedroom getting dressed for dinner. I had watched the rehearsal earlier in the day and he was supposed to say, "Coming," when his daughter told him dinner was ready. She didn't know he was not even on the set. Off camera, I yelled, "Give me ten minutes," as the camera was showing the bedroom door.

The stage manager yelled, "Cut," and everyone froze. "Where the hell is he?"

One of the stagehands said, "I think I saw him down the hall watching another show." I went down the hall and found him walking out of his friend's rehearsal to another show. I escorted him to the set and the live show continued.

The other event I must share happened when a well-known actor was playing the part of a macho detective. The detective was required to move quickly from one set to another. He had poor eyesight and wouldn't wear his glasses on set, so my job was to lead him from one set to another, off-camera, of course.

The show was a big success, and he thanked me and said the standard thing to say in

Hollywood—"Let me know if I can do anything for you!"—which is soon forgotten.

But this time, it meant a chance for a part in a new TV series, which was hosted each week by a different well-known actor. In this case, the actor was Dana Andrews, one of my favorites.

My reading was set for the next Monday, and I had a lot of lines. I wasn't good at cold reading and was very nervous, but the director expected that and told me to relax. Then he said the magic words: "You will be fine, but we have to cut that hair. You will be an Army sergeant, so you need to look like one. Come back in the morning and pick up your script and rehearsal schedule."

As soon as I left his office, I went to the telephone and called all the members of my family and a few others back in New Mexico.

The next day, I went to the director's office to get my TV script and rehearsal schedule. When I arrived at the office, I informed the secretary why I was there. She said, "Oh, that part was given to another actor this morning."

To say that I was devastated would be putting it mildly. I was a failure as an actor.

My job at NBC continued to be exciting. I met many fine actors and entertainers, but my acting career wasn't going anywhere. I had a few spots on local TV and some stage acting, but I needed to make a living.

Working around so many actors whom I had always admired was quite a thrill for a would-be actor, but I soon realized that Hollywood was full of handsome young men and beautiful young women, most of them with more talent than I had.

> "You can take all the sincerity in Hollywood, place it in the navel of a fruit fly, and still have room enough for three caraway seeds and a producer's heart."
> —Fred Allen

From the Canady Photo Collection

Above left: Gordon MacRae was Bob's favorite of all the entertainers and other famous people he encountered while working as a page at the NBC Studio. Above right: World-famous singer Jeanette MacDonald arrived at the studio in a Rolls-Royce limousine and Bob was asked to escort her into the studio.

From the Canady Photo Collection

Bob Canady had his résumé and glamor shot ready when he went to Hollywood to become an actor.

From the Canady Photo Collection

Bob Canady worked as a page on the Tennessee Ernie Ford show at the NBC Studio.

9
Finally, a Film and a Wife

The next page in the Hollywood chapters of my life came when I went to my acting class with Mildred Carr. Just as I considered giving up on the acting profession, two men who had seen me in a play came to the studio where I was working with Mildred. They asked if I would be interested in the leading role in a documentary they were making for the Greek Orthodox Church. Mildred had told them about me and convinced them I was best for the part. I thought, "Wow, where have I heard that before?"

I read for the part, and in less than an hour, I was a professional actor. This also meant I would be getting a share of the profits if there were any. I was assured that the film would be shown to thousands of people and could be used to get larger parts.

In Hollywood, the first thing that one needs to be considered for a TV or movie role is a sample of your acting that they can see on film. I agreed to do the part for no pay except for a copy of the film and a share of the profits.

The Greek Orthodox gentlemen were wonderful to us, and we were invited to shoot scenes in their homes. Of course, there were extra benefits to filming without pay. The food was delicious, and I probably gained ten pounds during the filming.

The film was called *The Orthodox Road*. It was made to show the problems that existed at the time when a member of the church married a person who was not a Greek Orthodox member.

> "No good movie is too long and no bad movie is short enough."
> —Roger Ebert

Before the film was finished, those of us who had professional exposure knew that the project was amateurish. We were not likely to see any money from it and knew we could never use it to gain professional exposure.

However, the making of the film did result in another important chapter of my life.

In the film was a beautiful young actress from the drama department at the University of Southern California to play my wife. Like me, Elaine was talented but had no professional experience. The only thing we had in common was a fantasy of being a movie star.

We weren't surprised when the film was finished that it was a terrible flop. Unfortunately, we refused to believe that our acting was also terrible. We were both stage-struck and determined to make it as professional actors. We knew some actors who were married, which seemed to help their careers. We continued to play our roles, and the dramatic thing we could think to do was to go to Las Vegas like "real" movie stars and get married. The young lady who was my wife in the film became my real wife.

Even before we returned to Los Angeles, I knew we had made a huge mistake. For Elaine, this was a real-life movie. I suddenly realized that, to her, life was a continual drama, and she could write her own script. A lesson from a freshman psychology course came to mind: "I'll believe it when I see it," versus "I'll see it when I believe it." She believed that reality only existed in her mind and, therefore, she could change it with her mind. I had married a total stranger.

10
VA Calling

Two days after we returned to Los Angeles, I received a formal letter from the Veterans Administration. It informed me that if I wasn't enrolled in college within the next six weeks, I would lose the remainder of my GI Bill benefits.

The notice came in the middle of the term at all colleges. There was no way I could be enrolled in six weeks. I went to Los Angeles City College to register but had no luck. As I walked out of the registrar's office, a young lady who worked there rushed up to me and told me about a small college in Orange County that was on a unique system. They held classes all morning long for six weeks at a time.

I drove to Chapman College and learned that it was a private school, very expensive, and only accepted students with an impressive scholastic record. I had nothing to lose, so I sat with the registrar at Chapman and told her my sad story. She agreed that Chapman College probably wasn't the place for me, but she had a wonderful idea. She could let me register for the next six-week term so I could renew my GI Bill benefits, and then I could register at Long Beach City College at the beginning of its next term.

> **The GI Bill was one of the most impactful, and one of the last, pieces of New Deal legislation. By 1956, the GI Bill had helped 7.8 million veterans further their education, some 2.2 million to attend colleges or universities, and an additional 5.6 million for some kind of training program.**
> —https://fdr.blogs.archives.gov/2020/11/10/fdr-gi-bill/

When she learned that I was married with a baby on the way, she decided I would certainly qualify for a hardship scholarship to pay for one semester at Chapman. I will forever be grateful for that wonderful woman.

I soon learned that one of the reasons I was allowed to enroll at Chapman College was that they had few veterans and even fewer art students. I learned more about art in that six-week period than I had in my entire life. In fact, my success in art was rewarded with a scholarship to Long Beach City College that made it possible for me to complete my degree in art education and become an art teacher at a local junior high school. By the time I completed my degree, we had three children—a girl, a boy, and another girl.

Art was a high priority in California at the time, and I was given all the supplies I wanted, including a kiln for ceramics, which appealed to junior high students.

Paintings by Dr. Canady

Photo above: Dr. Canady painted this watercolor of the San Juan Capistrano Mission near San Diego while he was owner and director of the Montessori School in Santa Barbara, California.

Photo at right: Having grown up in the Southwest, Dr. Canady has always enjoyed painting the mountains and desert landscape. After he moved to Tennessee, his focus became the valleys and mountains of East Tennessee.

Photos of Dr. Canady's paintings by Dr. Shirley Raines

Paintings by Dr. Canady

Photo below: This is Dr. Canady's favorite painting, an acrylic titled 'Road into the Smoky Mountains,' created for First United Methodist Church, Creativity Exhibit, 2015, in Oak Ridge, Tennessee.

Paintings by Dr. Canady

Photo above: This watercolor of the Portland Head Light, a lighthouse in Cape Elizabeth, near Portland Harbor in Maine, was painted in 2005 from a photo while in Memphis, Tennessee. The spray looks like an angel, which is not found in the photo. Photo at left: Dr. Canady painted this acrylic in remembrance of the Gilchrist Ranch (2010) where he worked in the summer as a hand. The painting is of sunrise at the ranch. A figure in the lower left is Bob drinking coffee before the other cowboys woke up.

Paintings by Dr. Canady

Photo at left: Dr. Canady painted the Quaking Aspens in 1984 after driving through Colorado.

Photo above: At age eighteen, Bob Canady created this oil painting of a Native American woman who spoke at Western New Mexico University in Silver City. She posed because Bob was an art student and a football player.

Paintings by Dr. Canady

Photo above: Dr. Canady created this acrylic painting of a ranch and mountains in a Southwestern native motif to illustrate light and shadow on the mountains in 2015 in Oak Ridge, Tennessee. Photo at right: He loved the fall colors that he painted in this view of the Smoky Mountains in autumn.

Paintings by Dr. Canady

Photo below: Dr. Canady created this oil painting of his wife, Dr. Shirley Raines, sitting on a catamaran on a resort beach near Fort Myers in 1993.

Part Three

Montessori Education and Lab School

Dr. Maria Montessori opened the first Montessori school—the Casa dei Bambini, or Children's House—in Rome on January 6, 1907.
Photo from Library of Congress

From the Canady Photo Collection

Dr. Bob Canady met Joanne Woodward and Paul Newman through the Montessori school that their children attended. Joanne Woodward's daughter was in Dr. Canady's youngest daughter's classroom at the Montessori school. Woodward invited them to her child's birthday party at the children's park in Beverly Hills.

11
Learning About Montessori Education

Another life-changing event occurred when my oldest daughter was five. She came home from her first day of kindergarten crying her eyes out. When I finally got her to tell me what was wrong, she said her teacher told her not to bring a book to school anymore. "You will learn to read in the first grade," the teacher said.

All of California was immersed in a phonics-first reading program, which discouraged parents from letting their children read until they had mastered the sounds of the letters. I still can't believe such a program existed.

I discussed this with one of the parents at a school meeting and he asked if I had ever heard of Maria Montessori. I hadn't. He suggested I read Montessori's book explaining her approach to early childhood education.

I borrowed the book from the library and stayed up most of the night reading about an incredible approach to early childhood education. I could see in my own young children everything she described about how children learn to read naturally. She was not only explaining the natural learning process, but she also developed materials to aid children.

I was so excited about this new concept that I took a couple of sick leave days, loaded up the family in my station wagon, and headed for the nearest Montessori school, which was in Santa Monica. I had called the director ahead of time and arranged a meeting.

When we arrived at the school, my wife took the children to a wonderful playground next to the school while I met with the director. He gave me a brief history of the school and then took me to some of the classrooms. I was amazed that the children kept right on doing what they were working on and paid no attention to us. I had to see for myself the deep concentration of children as they worked on individual pieces of Montessori apparatus, just as she had described in her book. The teacher gave a demonstration of each educational tool, and then the children were free to use it whenever and for as long as they wished.

Famous Montessori students in technology, engineering, and business:
- Katherine Graham, Pulitzer Prize-winning author and former owner and editor of the *Washington Post*
- Jeff Bezos, founder of Amazon
- Larry Page and Sergey Brin, founders of Google
- Peter Drucker, economic and business guru

—https://lifetimemontessorischool.com/what-famous-people-went-montessori-school

My excitement about Montessori education was evident when we returned to the director's office. The director told me that if I was interested in becoming a Montessori teacher or administrator, the school was beginning a class after the public-school year.

On the way home, I told my wife that I was going to resign from the junior high school where I was teaching, and we would be moving to Santa Monica. My wife, who always loved anything that was considered out of the norm, was excited about Montessori education, not because she understood it but because it was different.

The next day, at my junior high school, I told the principal that I would be resigning at the end of the school year. To my surprise, he was familiar with Montessori education and thought that it was a good idea.

I cashed in my retirement pay, and we moved to a small, inexpensive apartment in Santa Monica near the school. People taking the Montessori training program were able to enroll their children in the school at a reduced rate. My wife and I both got part-time jobs in the evening at the Santa Monica hospital.

Of course, the children loved the school and received a wonderful foundation for future education. The parents who enrolled their children were some of the top movie stars and celebrities. Parents Night at the school resembled a small awards night. It was a strange feeling to sit next to the celebrities and share stories about our children.

One of the actors asked me who my daughter's dressmaker was. I laughed and said, "My mother makes all of her clothes."

Joanne Woodward, whose daughter was in my youngest daughter's classroom, invited my daughter to her child's birthday party at the children's park

Famous Montessori students in the arts:
- Gabriel Garcia Marquez, Nobel Prize-winning novelist
- Joshua Bell, Grammy Award-winning violinist
- George Clooney, Academy Award-winning actor, director, producer, and humanitarian
- Beyonce Knowles, singer, songwriter, and sixteen-time Grammy winner
- Yo-Yo Ma, cellist and winner of fifteen Grammy Awards and the Presidential Medal of Freedom
- Taylor Swift, Grammy-winning singer/songwriter and Entertainer of the Year
- Dakota Fanning, actress and Screen Actors Award nominee
- John and Joan Cusack, brother and sister actors

—https://lifetimemontessorischool.com/what-famous-people-went-montessori-school

in Beverly Hills. I took my daughter to the party, where a greeter met us at the gate and told me to pick her up at three in the afternoon.

When I went back to pick up my daughter, she was over by the carousel, which had little sports cars instead of horses. She was the only one on the carousel. When she came around to me, I started to lift her off when I heard a loud voice saying, "Who are you?"

When I turned around, I saw Joanne Woodward, who then smiled and said, "You're her father. Come on over to the table so we can talk."

My daughter went with another attendant, and I went to the table with Joanne Woodward to converse with Paul Newman and two other fathers from the Montessori school. The conversation was a serious one about organizing a whole new church. As we were ending the conversation, Newman's oldest son came over and asked for some money to play at the shooting gallery. Newman reached into the pocket of his expensive jeans and drew out a large roll of bills, peeled off two twenties, and waved his son off to the shooting arcade. It was quite a macho display.

Another memorable incident at the school occurred when Marlon Brando was sitting on a bench near the playground while his son played with my son. I sat down next to him while he held a large German shepherd puppy. Suddenly, the dog jumped out of Brando's arms, ran over to his little boy, and knocked him down, causing the child to cry. Brando jumped up, rushed over, picked up his son, and in a baby-talk voice said, "That's all right, sweetheart." Then, in a rough, tough voice, he said, "Bad dog! Bad dog." I will never forget this macho Marlon Brando's sensitivity and gentle voice reassuring his son.

One other incident needs to be mentioned. A movie star arrived in an expensive sports car to get his child. We were surprised, because his son's nanny had already picked him up. I went out to the car and told him someone else had picked up his son. We both looked at each other and panicked. The children's safety was my responsibility.

The actor was terrified because we thought the child might have been abducted, a worry of many movie stars. I cautioned him not to panic until we called his home to find out if anyone there knew who picked up the child a few minutes early from the school. The actor found out the nanny had gotten his child, but he warned me, "Never, never let anyone you don't know pick up my son."

From the Canady Photo Collection

Dr. Canady was sitting on a bench at the school playground with Marlon Brando, who held his German shepherd puppy in his lap. The puppy ran over and knocked down Brando's son. The famous actor rushed to comfort his son with baby talk.

From the Canady Photo Collection

Dr. Canady was invited to sit at the table with Joanne Woodward, Paul Newman, and two other dads at a child's birthday party. The topic then was founding a new church.

12
My Own Montessori School

When I completed the training program at the Santa Monica Montessori school, I decided to start my own Montessori school. I discussed the possibility with two teachers, and we agreed to open a new school in Santa Barbara, California. Both teachers came from Ireland and were strictly trained in Montessori education.

The two teachers and I arranged for a meeting with some prominent citizens of Santa Barbara who had young children or grandchildren who were three to five years old. We held the meeting in a private beach club where we had a meal and conducted the meeting near the swimming pool. When we arrived, we were pleased to find more parents and grandparents than we expected. We took turns explaining Montessori education as a means of early childhood education. We explained that we would open the Montessori school at the old University of California campus overlooking the water.

The reaction was better than we expected. At the end of the meeting, we had enrolled

> From its humble beginnings more than a hundred years ago as a single schoolroom for a group of underprivileged children in Rome, Italy, Montessori education has taken a firm foothold on the education landscape. In the US alone, approximately 5,000 Montessori schools now serve over one million children, from infancy through adolescence. Thousands more Montessori schools exist worldwide.
> —https://amshq.org/About-Montessori/History-of-Montessori

twenty-five children. A woman gave us a check for her grandchildren's entire year of tuition, and she convinced others to do the same. From that meeting, we had enough financing to launch the school.

The school grew quickly, and soon we expanded from one classroom to four. Each classroom had an observation room where visitors could come and go without disturbing the children.

13
Surprise Visitor Leads to Career Change

One day, after returning from a meeting downtown, I was told that a university professor was waiting in my office. He introduced himself and told me he was impressed with what he saw at the school and wondered if I would be interested in a position at his university. He said that he would be interested in doing some research on using Montessori education in Head Start programs. I told him that Dr. Montessori's concepts originated with young children in the slums of Rome.

> "All that I am, or hope to be, I owe to my angel mother."
> —Abraham Lincoln

I was immediately interested in what he was proposing, and I asked him what his university was. His response was quite a shock to me. He came from a university I attended after leaving the Air Force. He was referring to the college near my hometown where I had attended and where my brothers had graduated.

> Early Head Start and Head Start regulations allow mixed-aged classrooms. Therefore, as long as the specific requirements for each age group are met or exceeded, Head Start and Early Head Start grants can be extended to a Montessori program. Head Start regulations do cap class size at between fifteen and twenty children for pre-K and kindergarten students, depending on the ages of the children in the classroom.
> —11 Head Start Program, 45 CFR § 1301-1305 (2015). https://www.public-montessori.org/wp-content/uploads/2022/02/Head-Start-Early-Head-Start-and-Montessori.pdf

I told him that I would certainly think about it and let him know.

That night, I couldn't go to sleep, thinking about the incredible coincidence. My children had reached the age where it was time to leave the Montessori school and go to public school, and I was beginning to tire of being in a supervisory role that I was uncomfortable doing. But what made the final decision for me was that my mother was in poor health, and I needed to be near her.

I slept well that night after becoming convinced that I wanted to join the professor at his university. The next morning, I called and asked him for more information about what position I would have at the university. He said I would be teaching a combination third- and fourth-grade class at the university's Lab School and conducting seminars on Montessori education for university students and Head Start teachers.

The professor added that I would need a master's degree, but I could get that through night classes. I told him that I wasn't sure I would be accepted in the master's program because my transcript wasn't very impressive. He assured me that I would be accepted and would have no problem with the coursework.

A lawyer who had children in the Montessori school took over the school, and soon the Canady family was on the way to a new adventure in New Mexico.

14
Back to New Mexico

The combination third- and fourth-grade class at the University Lab School was mostly boys. Their learning abilities ranged from very low to very high. I soon learned that their former teacher had resigned in frustration. Four fourth-grade boys with severe learning problems had been disrupting the whole class.

On my first day of class, I was standing at the front of the room introducing myself when one of the four boys, who was obviously the leader, came right up to me and said, "Mr. Canady, this is really a tough class. If you have any trouble, I'll be glad to help."

I pointed to his desk and said, "You get back to your desk and don't ever interrupt me again!"

I created various learning centers, and the children quickly learned that they could complete the work in the centers at their own pace, and they loved it. Each center was designed, not only with materials for independent learning, but also for students to test their own progress. They knew that I would test them periodically and there was little cheating. Two student teachers from the university who weren't familiar with the learning center concept learned quickly how and when to help individual children.

Once the classroom was operating smoothly, I found time to work individually with the four boys. I soon found that they were not slow learners; they were victims of beginning reading instruction that didn't work for them. I realized that I had four students who, as my former professor would say, were right-brained learners in a left-brain reading program.

At home that night, I created a furry little cartoon character who wore a cowboy hat and rode an eight-cylinder motorcycle. I looked at him and decided the only name for him was "Macho."

The first stories I wrote were about him arriving in Silver City, New Mexico, and popping a wheelie right in front of the Lab School before cruising Broadway in the middle of town. I had the office secretary make five copies of the picture and the story. I gave a copy to each boy and read the story to them as they followed along. Their response was even more dramatic than I had anticipated. One of the boys even glanced out the window like he was expecting to see Macho.

They took turns reading the story to each other. I went to the other side of the room and appeared to be helping a group of children, but when I glanced over at the boys, one of them was correcting the reader about a particular word.

I told the boys that when each one could read the story without any mistakes, I would give them the next Macho story. I wasn't surprised when they all could read the story and identify each word individually.

Each day, I gave the secretary a new story, which the boys decided to call "The Adventures of Macho." Macho's adventures took place in various areas of town, and the boys were soon writing their own stories, which they reluctantly read to the whole class.

I wasn't surprised by the interest shown by the other children in the Lab School, but

I was a little surprised when a boy who came from the poorest area of Silver City wanted to take one of the new stories I had written home with him. I told him he knew the rules; he couldn't take a story home until we had read it in class.

"Well, OK," he said. "But my dad is sure going to be disappointed."

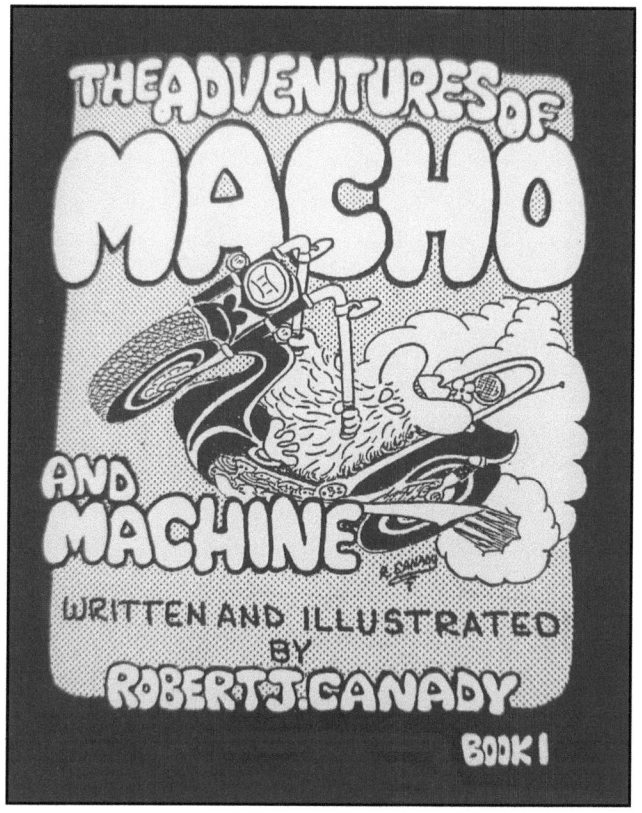

From the Canady Photo Collection

Bob Canady created a book called *The Adventures of Macho and Machine* to help improve his students' reading skills.

Canady Macho books for young readers

From the Canady Photo Collection

Photo above: Dr. Canady teaches reading to a group of boys using the book he created for them called *The Adventures of Macho and Machine*. Photos at right: His second book was *The Adventures of Macho and Mimi*.

Part Four

Dr. Canady, Professor

Dr. Canady's abstract dissertation was on the topic 'Consistency of Teachers' Methods of Teaching Reading to Specific Learning Theories.'

Bob Canady returned to Western New Mexico University, where he began his undergraduate studies, to pursue his master's degree.
Photo courtesy of Western New Mexico University

Photo courtesy of Western New Mexico University

Bob Canady taught a combination third- and fourth-grade class at Western New Mexico University's Lab School and conducted seminars on Montessori education for university students and Head Start teachers.

From the Canady Photo Collection

Bob Canady graduated in 1971 with a master's degree from Western New Mexico University.

15
From Lab School in Silver City to a University

The success of the Macho stories led to another chapter in my life. A professor from the University of Arizona who was visiting town heard about my classroom and asked to observe it. I was pleased to have him. After school, we had an interesting conversation. He asked if I was familiar with Dr. Van Allen at the University of Arizona. I told him I wasn't, and he described the work the professor was doing in what was called the language experience approach, which included children learning to read from their own stories that they told or dictated to the teacher. He felt that children should understand the association between the spoken word and the written word and be involved with the process of reading before being taught the sounds each letter makes.

In simple terms, children should learn to read by reading their own words. The children who are read to at home and who have been involved in the reading process are more likely to understand a "skills-first" approach to reading instruction. Children who have not been read to are confused when they are asked what sound a letter makes or expected to memorize words out of context.

I agreed with everything I was told about Dr. Allen's approach to reading instruction and wanted to learn more. The professor said that he would arrange for me to meet with Dr. Allen if I could come to Tucson. We agreed on a particular day, and before long, I was sitting in Dr. Allen's beautiful, Spanish-style home in the foothills of Tucson.

As we shared ideas about our approach to reading instruction, I was shocked when he suddenly suggested that I come to Tucson and become his doctoral student.

> "Travel stories teach geography; insect stories lead the child into natural science, and so on. The teacher, in short, can use reading to introduce her pupils to the most varied subjects, and the moment they have been thus started, they can go on to any limit guided by the single passion for reading."
> —Maria Montessori

My excitement ended when I realized that with my poor academic record, I would never be admitted to a doctoral program. I reluctantly told him about my poor record and how I had been accepted on probation to my undergraduate and master's programs.

He was surprised but not shocked and said, "Standardized tests were never kind to creative people. If you don't mind being on probation one more time, I can assure you that you will be accepted."

The doctoral committee wasn't as understanding as Dr. Allen, but they reluctantly accepted me on probation. I later learned that they were envious of Dr. Allen's international reputation. They accepted me hoping I would fail and smear his reputation.

Dr. Allen discovered that I would have a financial problem moving my family to Tucson and finding housing until my house in Silver City was sold. This wonderful man paid for a nice house for us in Tucson with the understanding that I could pay him back when my house sold. Then he arranged for me to teach two classes at the university and receive pay as an assistant professor. I didn't let him down and excelled in my coursework and in my teaching.

My doctoral committee members decided to take one final shot at Dr. Allen during the defense of my dissertation. The dissertation was well written, and the only criticism they could find of my study was that it was an idea that Dr. Allen had suggested. After an hour of nitpicking, the only member of the committee who had become friendly with me said, "OK, enough already. We know we are going to approve his dissertation, and I have papers to grade, so let's get on with it."

I was asked to leave the room, and fifteen minutes later, Dr. Allen came to me, shook my hand, and said, "Congratulations, Dr. Canady." I decided that kissing him probably wasn't a good idea.

During my doctoral program, I also had the opportunity to study with two other internationally known professors who were leaders in the field of psycholinguistics. They were doing research concerning the reading process—in other words, what happens physically and mentally when a person reads. Although most of their work was over my head, one thing was made clear—reading is a "whole-to-part" process, and reading instruction should also be approached from a "whole-to-part" perspective.

Photos by Dan Rountree, Tuscaloosa, Alabama

Above left: Dr. Shirley Raines and Dr. Bob Canady were married on March 10, 1979. Above right: Immediately after the wedding, they posed for another photo with Shirley's son Brian, then age nine.

16
From Tucson to Tuscaloosa

With Dr. Allen's help, I was able to construct an attractive résumé and soon had job offers at several major universities. One was the University of Alabama.

I owed a lot to my football experience and "Bear" Bryant had just won the national championship. My decision was easy: "I'm going with the Bear."

I boarded an airplane in the dry summer heat of Phoenix, Arizona, and landed in the humid heat of Tuscaloosa, Alabama. I felt like I had landed in the middle of a jungle. Everything in Arizona was brown and gray and dry, but it was wet and green in Alabama. I decided if Bear was here, it couldn't be too bad.

I soon found that the head of the university's education department was the only faculty member who was excited about "whole-language" reading instruction and the language experience approach. Others considered it a fad and thought it would soon go away.

When I expressed my concerns to the department head, he said, "That's why you are here—to bring new life to the early childhood program and to offer leadership to the teachers of young children." After a short time working with the faculty and the early childhood teachers who attended the night classes, I could see that change was a concept that was difficult for them to embrace.

I was encouraged when I began getting numerous requests to speak to groups throughout the state. I was even asked to go into classrooms and conduct demonstration lessons with children. I learned that the schools were interested in using the government money they were given for in-service training.

After several years of feeling that I was wasting my time, I was ready for a change. The change came in the form of a beautiful young woman who had just finished her doctorate in early childhood education at the University of Tennessee. We needed another faculty member for the early childhood program and invited her to interview for the position.

During our first conversation, we realized that we were on the same page where early childhood education was concerned. I had finally found someone who was familiar with Dr. Allen's work and the "whole-language" approach to reading instruction.

By the time she left the campus, I knew I had just met a special person and an early childhood colleague. The dean of the college asked what I thought of the candidate for the job, and I said, "We better grab her if we can get her." She accepted our offer, and a new chapter of my life began.

My youngest child had just graduated from high school, and my wife and I had agreed to end our marriage, as planned. She fulfilled a longtime fantasy of hers and entered law school.

Meanwhile, I set out to improve our early childhood program with the help of our new faculty member, Dr. Shirley Raines. She also was recently divorced, and it came as no surprise to anyone that our close professional relationship also became a close personal relationship. We set our first date for a Friday night. Later that day, I received a letter in my box from Bear Bryant.

Back then, the school had a custom that two faculty members were invited to each home football game. I asked how one was chosen. One faculty member looked at another and said, "He'll find out."

At the time I received the letter, I had two All-American football players in one of my early childhood classes. One player was an outstanding student, but the other was failing the class. I met with him after class and advised him to drop the course because he wasn't going to pass it. In less than a week, I received a letter from Bear inviting me to be his guest at the next football game. I asked the dean what I should do about the invitation and he said, "Go and enjoy the game and give the student whatever he deserves."

I thought the problem was solved until I realized I was expected to have dinner with the team on Friday evening—the evening of my first date with Shirley.

Shirley still jokes about competing with Bear Bryant and losing. But we both won and have enjoyed a continuing date for over forty wonderful years.

> "Winning isn't everything, but it beats anything that comes in second."
> —Bear Bryant

Shirley had been successful in various administrative roles before coming to Alabama, and when the head of the education department resigned, she was asked to fill the position. She reluctantly agreed but knew she was being asked because no one else wanted the job. She did her best to bring a fragmented faculty together to work as a team.

After one frustrating year, we knew that it was time for us to move on. We had both been offered positions at universities where they were familiar with our concepts of a successful early childhood program and successful reading programs.

I had done two workshops at Northeastern State University in Oklahoma, stressing the use of language experience and the "whole-language" approach to reading instruction. The workshops were attended by a large group of classroom teachers and university students who were planning to be elementary school teachers.

I was excited about the way my ideas were accepted. On the way to the airport for my flight back, the head of the education department said the magic words. He asked, "How much money would it take to get someone like you to join our faculty and restructure our reading program?"

I was tempted to say, "I'll come for free!" Instead, I told him that I would come as a full professor and there must be a position for Shirley. He agreed, and soon Shirley and I were moving into a new house in Tahlequah, Oklahoma.

However, I must add an incident that showed Shirley's resolve. When we first arrived at Northeastern for a meeting with the dean, he welcomed me warmly and barely talked with Shirley. Near the end of the conversation, he said that they were excited to have me, but unfortunately, they could only provide a three-quarter position for Shirley, not a full-time position. Shirley calmly rose from her chair and said, "Bob, come on, we are leaving. You and I both were promised full-time positions. Let's go."

I excused us from the dean's office and left. By the time I got to the hallway, Shirley was rapidly descending the stairs, not waiting for the elevator on the third floor. At that point, the dean rushed out of the door to his office and invited me to come back in. Shirley overheard what was going on but did not return to the dean's office. I am happy to report that by the time she had gotten to our car, the dean had decided there would be a full-time position for my wife, as promised.

Shirley was hired as a full-time supervisor of student teachers. I was finally able to structure a beginning reading program for early childhood teachers based on all I had learned from mentors and my own experience with small children.

Tahlequah, Oklahoma, is the western headquarters of the Cherokee Nation, and the Cherokee education students found that this new approach to reading instruction was especially successful with small Cherokee children.

Dr. Canady drew this cartoon of legendary University of Alabama football coach Bear Bryant.

Planes I Have Enjoyed Flying

Photo at top right: Dr. Canady flew this Piper 140. In 1988, he flew his Piper 140 from Manassas, Virginia, to Kitty Hawk, North Carolina, to the Wright Brothers Museum. The same airplane was flown from Manassas to Toronto, Ontario, Canada. On Bob's return flight, he stopped in Buffalo, New York, for customs. Later in the flight, he encountered a dangerous storm over the mountains of Pennsylvania on May 2, 1988. By the grace of God, he landed the plane on a 5,000-foot runway at Mifflin County (Pennsylvania) Airport. Photo at bottom left: Dr. Canady flew this Cessna 172 purchased in 1989 and continued to fly until he gave up his pilot's license in 2002.

Photos from the Canady Photo Collection

Planes I Have Enjoyed Flying

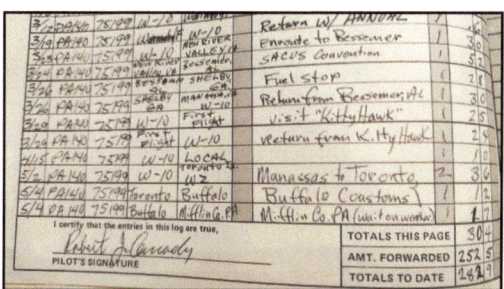

Bob started taking flying lessons in 1985 from Cecil T. Hammons when Bob was living in Tahlequah, Oklahoma. Lessons were in a Cessna 150, Cessna 152, Cherokee Beech Muskie, and Piper 140. Later, he owned a Cessna 150 and Piper, among others. The pilot's log at left shows the date of the flight from Toronto to Mifflin, Pennsylvania, where Bob almost crashed during a storm.

Photos from the Canady Photo Collection

Photo courtesy of Ken LaRock and the National Museum of the USAF

The Lockheed VC-121E Columbine III is displayed at the National Museum of the United States Air Force in Dayton, Ohio, on April 23, 2016. This aircraft is one of ten presidential aircraft in the collection. The museum is open daily from 9 a.m. to 5 p.m. and has free admission and parking. Dr. Canady became enthralled with flying and airplanes as a USAF air policeman. One of his bucket-list items is to visit the museum and see the restored Columbine, which was used as Air Force One.

17
Learning to Fly in Tahlequah

People assume that I learned to fly in the Air Force. However, I learned to fly at a small public airport northeast of Tahlequah, Oklahoma, while I was teaching at Northeastern State University.

While there in 1985, I ventured to the airport and met Cecil T. Hammons. I'll never forget the day we met. I walked into the airport and saw an older gentleman sitting at a long table with his leg propped up on a chair, drinking coffee. "Anyone around here a flight instructor?" I said.

"Why do you want to know?" he asked in a gruff voice.

I proceeded with a story or two about wanting to learn to fly and then said, "I don't expect instructors take people like me," pointing to my gray hair. "I'm fifty-three years old. Guess I'm too old to learn to fly."

Cecil replied, "Well, if you think a man twenty years older than you can teach you to fly, we might be able to sign you up today for a trial flight and let you decide whether you want to learn to fly or not. Some folks think they want to fly until I take them up and let them take the controls of the plane, and they get the feel of it."

"Oh, sir, I want to learn to fly. I've been dreaming about it since my Air Force days," I answered.

I followed Cecil out to a Cessna 152, equipped as a trainer. As promised, he let me take the controls. From that day forward, I was hooked on flying. Side-by-side, shoulder-to-shoulder, he taught and I practiced during the ten lessons that followed.

"Canady," he would say, "You have a good sense of where you are in the air, but you gotta rely on your instruments, man." We practiced maneuvers rigorously, sometimes blindfolded. I could look down at the instruments, not out at the sky. Stalls, forced landings, cross-country, water landings with a platoon plane, Cecil taught me everything until one day, he slammed the door of the Cessna 150 and said, "Get out of here; go fly solo."

> "It is the greatest shot of adrenaline to be doing what you have wanted to do so badly. You almost feel like you could fly without the plane."
> —Charles Lindbergh

To date, I have owned six airplanes—two Cessnas, two Pipers, one Beechcraft, and one ERCO Coupe, or Air Coupe, a small plane with a retractable dome over the cockpit that feels like you are flying a fighter plane.

With Shirley as the navigator and me as the pilot, we airport-hopped across Arkansas, Tennessee, Texas, New Mexico, and Arizona from our home base in Tahlequah. We flew to the Outer Banks and Kitty Hawk, North Carolina, from our home in Fairfax, Manassas Airport. We bought a vacation house in Norris, Tennessee, and flew there often to be with Shirley's son, Brian, who was living in Oak Ridge. From our home in Tampa, we flew to small coastal towns around Florida. I flew to conferences for presentations in my role as a professor at Marymount University in Arlington, Virginia. One such reading conference in Toronto proved to be a turning point in my life.

Every two years, I had my biannual flight checkup, including for medical conditions, private pilot lessons renewal training on instruments, and visual. I never tackled the instrument rating, even though I had some training.

We enjoyed our time in Tahlequah for four years, but we were looking for opportunities for Shirley to get back into the university classroom as a professor rather than a supervisor of student teachers. I felt that I had established a reading program that would be continued even after I left.

When Shirley was offered an interesting position on the faculty at George Mason University in Fairfax, Virginia, I told her that she should accept it and I would find a job somewhere in the area.

Shortly after we arrived in Fairfax, I learned of an opening on the faculty of Marymount University in Arlington, Virginia, near Washington, DC. To my amazement, when I contacted the dean of the college of education, she knew about me. She had read my articles in the *Reading Teacher* and had seen the film I developed about the language experience approach. She said, "Of course, the position is yours if you want it, and a full professorship is no problem."

I didn't realize that Marymount University would be the last university where I would teach and the most enjoyable teaching experience of my career. The undergraduate students were bright and eager to learn, but my favorites were the students in the evening classes. They were men and women who held degrees in areas other than education and were working on their master's degrees in education to become teachers. They were second-career people who had always wanted to be teachers and were finally working toward their goals. But they were apprehensive about facing students in a classroom. I had to be careful about what I said in the class because they seemed to be writing down every word.

The most memorable experience of my time at Marymount originated from a naval officer who attended one of my night courses. After class one night, he came up to me with a wonderful suggestion. He said, "You know, Dr. Canady, if you could teach a class over at the Pentagon, you could fill the room with men who are leaving the service and returning to civilian life. They just can't make it over here to come to class."

The next morning, I told the dean about the idea, and she thought it was great. She made a few phone calls, and the next thing I knew, I had an appointment with an important colonel at the Pentagon. I met the officer from my class at the entrance to the Pentagon, and he escorted me to my meeting with the colonel. It was a short meeting because the colonel was already sold on the idea and had arranged for a lecture room where the classes would be held. He also arranged for me to be escorted to an office where I filled out the forms necessary for entrance into the building and the classroom.

> "Once you have tasted flight, you will forever walk the earth with your eyes turned skyward, for there you have been, and there you will always long to return."
> —Leonardo da Vinci

Everything happened so fast that I was a little overwhelmed when the evening for the first class arrived. I found my parking place, showed my credentials, and was escorted to the classroom. I entered the room and put my materials on a table. When I turned around to face the room, I realized I was at the bottom of a large room with the tables and chairs placed on an incline on a curved wall. I was also facing more than forty military officers from all branches of the service and in full uniform.

The only thing I could think to say was, "Do you have any idea what it's like for me, an old, enlisted man, to look at all this 'brass' and expect to teach you something?"

My joke eased the tension in the room, and when the six Navy pilots in the class learned I was a private pilot, we all relaxed. I didn't realize when we occasionally swapped flying stories that an event in the air would soon make a dramatic change in my life.

Part Five

Pilot Meets God on 5,000-Foot Runway

Photo courtesy of Beth Reifsnyder, chairman, Mifflin County Airport Authority

The Mifflin County Airport in Mifflin, Pennsylvania, is the haven that Dr. Bob Canady found when he was flying in a severe storm after he had been a presenter at an international reading conference in Toronto, Ontario, Canada. Although he knew a storm front was headed for Pennsylvania, he believed that if he left right away, he would be ahead of it in his Piper 140. But the battery was dead on his plane, and the half-hour delay to charge the battery proved disastrous.

Photo courtesy of Beth Reifsnyder, chairman, Mifflin County Airport Authority

Dr. Canady did not have an instrument rating to fly, and when he saw storm clouds covering the mountaintops, he knew he had to land. He was losing visibility and had no place to land. He prayed and made a promise to God. Then he looked off his left-wing tip and saw a 5,000-foot runway. He banked the plane and made a perfect landing. He spent the night in the small terminal office at Mifflin County Airport, in Mifflin, Pennsylvania, where he was greeted warmly. As a result of his prayer, he began his stained-glass ministry some years later, creating more than eighty-five stained-glass windows for churches that could not afford them. Beth Reifsnyder, who offered the runway photos for this book, said, 'May Dr. Canady's legacy live on.'

18
The Flying Event That Changed My Life

I was scheduled to make a presentation at an international reading conference in Toronto, Ontario, Canada. I decided it would be fun to fly my plane there. The flight went smoothly, and I landed at a small airport near downtown Toronto with a short walk to the hotel and convention center.

Private pilots must always be aware of the weather, and I checked with flight service each morning. On the third morning, flight service informed me that a front was due to pass through Pennsylvania, but I should stay ahead of it if I left right away.

I checked out of the hotel and hurried to the airport, where I filled out my flight plan for a short flight to Buffalo, New York, where I would be cleared by customs. I climbed into my pretty Piper 140, stashed my suitcase, and reached for the key to start the engine. I was shocked to see that the key was not only already in the ignition, but I had left it on since the day I landed there. Of course, the battery was dead. This wasn't too serious at the time, but the half hour it took to recharge the battery turned out to be very serious.

I landed at the Buffalo airport thirty minutes later than expected and taxied up to the customs office. The officer in charge came over to the plane as I was getting out and said, "You were due in here forty-five minutes ago." Before I could explain about the dead battery, he said, "You better go inside and have a cup of coffee. This may take a while."

I suddenly realized what his concerns were. There had been several recent cases of drugs being smuggled out of Canada in small airplanes. The forty-five extra minutes that showed on his flight information could have looked like I might have landed somewhere and picked up some drugs.

After a thorough search of the plane, I was cleared to leave. When I checked with flight service, I was warned that the storm had entered Pennsylvania and would soon move into my flight path, but since I was already in the air, I should be able to stay ahead of it.

By the time I reached the first row of mountains in Pennsylvania, the storm was close behind me and the clouds kept getting lower. I flew over the first mountains and started across the valley to the mountains on the other side. By the time I reached the other side, the clouds had lowered and were covering the tops of the mountains. No pilot without an instrument rating would ever consider flying blind over a mountain. I quickly realized that I needed to turn around and get out of the valley.

When I started back, I soon discovered that the clouds were now covering the mountains behind me. I decided to see if I could fly down the valley and get out that way. I found that the visibility was even worse in that direction.

I had to find a clearing somewhere and put the plane down before I lost all visibility. I flew back up the valley, and the only possibility I found was a "drag strip," but I realized that it was surrounded by poles and wires, making an emergency landing impossible.

The next thing that happened to me can cost a pilot his life: I panicked! I was losing visibility and had no place to make a forced landing. I had never spoken a serious prayer in my life, but I decided it was all I had left. My prayer was nothing very dramatic, but it did clear my mind and I got control of the airplane. I also remembered that I had seen an interstate highway somewhere at the other end of the valley, which had been cut like a *V* in the mountain. If I could find it, I could land on the highway or at least lower the airplane and fly out of the valley under the clouds.

I found the interstate, but it was during the local rush hour and there was no way to put the airplane down without endangering innocent people, something a pilot should never do. But I was able to lower the airplane to stay just under the clouds and look for any flat place to make a forced landing. Just as I was beginning to feel better about my chances for survival, the black cloud above me opened up and the rain came down so hard that I couldn't see the nose of the airplane. My first thought was not only for my own life but for all the people on the freeway below me.

I did the only thing I had left—I said a prayer, this time out loud and very clearly. My exact words were, "Dear God, maybe you didn't hear me. I am in a lot of trouble. If you will help me get out of this trouble, I will do something wonderful in your name."

What happened next, most people would say was coincidence, but I know better.

When I looked off my left-wing tip, there was a 5,000-foot runway in the only visible clearing. I simply banked the plane and made a perfect landing.

I taxied up to the small terminal, got out of the airplane, raised my arms in the pouring rain, and said, "Thank you, God!"

Two men were standing under the cover of the terminal entrance, and one said, "Get in here. You're getting soaked!"

I said, "Yes, isn't it wonderful?"

I spent the night in the small terminal office. The next morning was bright and clear. I had them fill my gas tanks and then took a peaceful, uneventful trip back home to Virginia.

Now, one might assume that I would suddenly become a very religious person, but that didn't happen. Pilots are a rare breed. They believe they are indestructible. Why else would they get into a small airplane and fly over large mountains?

Rev. Quinten L. Smith, wearing black robes, and the choir at Greater Payne Chapel African Methodist Episcopal Church in Memphis, Tennessee, sing, 'He's got the whole world in his hands.' They added a verse, 'He's got Dr. Canady in his hands. He's got the whole world in his hands.'

Rev. Quinten L. Smith and Dr. Canady install a stained-glass window on the front of Greater Payne Chapel African Methodist Episcopal Church. The cross and the anvil are symbols of the church.
Photos by Mark Stansbury

Part Six

Stained-Glass Ministry

From the Canady Photo Collection

Dr. Canady installs windows at Canaan Baptist Church in Ashland, Mississippi, as church member Freddie Graves, now deceased, watches. The pastor is Brother Paul Adams.

Dr. Bob Canady and his wife, Dr. Shirley Raines, toured the Torpedo Factory Art Center in Alexandria, Virginia. When Bob visited a stained-glass studio, he was inspired to become a stained-glass artist. This eventually led to his ministry when he created more than eighty-five stained-glass windows for churches that could not afford them.

The Torpedo Factory Art Center is housed in a 100-year-old converted munitions plant that was built in 1918-1919. Today, several hundred artisans create in their studios in the Torpedo Factory Art Center, run by the City of Alexandria. The Art Center celebrated its fiftieth anniversary in 2023.

Photos courtesy of the Torpedo Factory (torpedofactory.org)

19
The Pilot Becomes an Artist Again

Before we left the Washington, DC, area, we visited the Torpedo Factory, a large warehouse building on the banks of the Potomac River. The converted factory housed more than 150 working artists in their studios. One of the studios featured stained glass. I had never been interested in stained glass because what little I knew about it seemed to resemble paint by numbers, a process I thought was simply buying a book of designs, cutting out the designs, using them as patterns for the glass, and then soldering them together to complete the ready-made design.

Above the door of the stained-glass studio was a sign saying, "Painting with Glass." The examples I saw were beautiful and unlike any stained-glass patterns that I had ever seen. I was hooked. I began working with stained glass, and that proved to make a difference in my life as an artist.

From Northern Virginia with my six years' time at Marymount and Shirley's at

George Mason, we moved to Tampa, Florida, for Shirley to continue her work as the chair of a large department of childhood, language arts, and reading with faculty on five different campuses. With her colleague chairs, deans, and other administrators, Shirley proved to be an outstanding administrator at the University of South Florida and enjoyed it immensely.

> "For me, a stained-glass window is a transparent partition between my heart and the heart of the world."
> —Marc Chagall

Meanwhile, I decided to consult with school districts around the country, but my heart was in returning to my art, particularly my interest in stained glass. I created several pieces for our home in Temple Terrace, including a large, curved, stained-glass window. I was hooked on the art medium and became engrossed in design, improving my skills, and learning as much as possible.

From the Canady Photo Collection

Dr. Canady created this curved, stained-glass window for his and Dr. Raines's home in Temple Terrace, Florida.

Trinity Hill Methodist Church Stained-Glass Windows

"I thought we were finished when the twenty-fourth window was installed in the sanctuary, but Shirley thought we should have a large window of Leonardo da Vinci's *The Last Supper* in the narthex. God must have been working again."

Trinity Hill Methodist Church Stained-Glass Windows

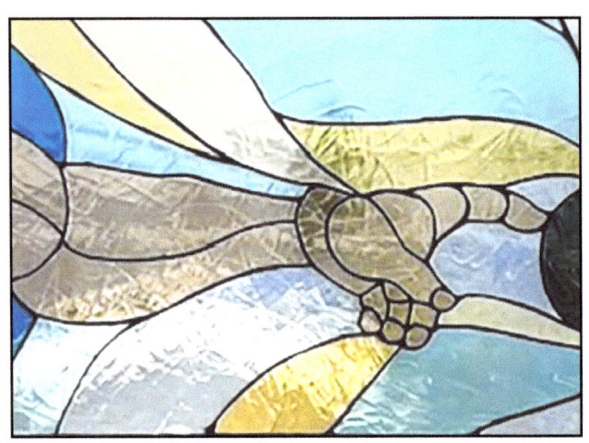

MOSES and THE BURNING BUSH
Exodus 3:1–6
Given by Ida Black
Memory of Loved Ones

CREATION
Genesis 1:1
Given by Chancel Choir
Memory of Joan Haddix

NOAH and THE ARK
Genesis 8:8, 9
Given by Bill Ashbrook
Honor of John & Pam
Stephenson and Family

Trinity Hill Methodist Church Stained-Glass Windows

Trinity Hill Methodist Church Stained-Glass Windows, Lexington, Kentucky

Trinity Hill Methodist Church Stained-Glass Windows

Trinity Hill Methodist Church Stained-Glass Windows

Trinity Hill Methodist Church Stained-Glass Windows

Trinity Hill Methodist Church Stained-Glass Windows

JESUS HEALING
Mark 5: 22-43
Given by Bud & Dot Brooks
Memory of Loved Ones

PRAYER IN THE GARDEN
Luke 22: 39-48
Given by Tom & Reva Brehm
In Memory of
Walter E. & Lucille Brehm

Trinity Hill Methodist Church Stained-Glass Windows

Trinity Hill Methodist Church Stained-Glass Windows

Trinity Hill Methodist Church Stained-Glass Windows

Dr. Robert Canady created more than eighty-five stained-glass windows in his gift to churches in Kentucky, Tennessee, and Mississippi.

Trinity Hill Methodist Church Stained-Glass Windows

20
New Position for Shirley, Artist Calling for Bob

When the University of Kentucky advertised the position of dean of the College of Education, I encouraged Shirley to apply. We both had been interested in the University of Kentucky and felt that the Lexington area would be a great place to live. It also was closer to Shirley's son, who lived approximately 150 miles away.

We were both thrilled when Shirley was selected. We were eager to move into our new home, which was near the beautiful Kentucky horse farms and Keeneland racecourse.

We soon found a Methodist church that we liked and invited the pastor to come to our house. He was delighted to learn that we wanted to join the church and was interested in a small glass window I had made for our dining room.

When he found that I was a stained-glass artist, he said I might be able to help him with a problem he was having at the church. He said that a group of members had formed a committee to explore the possibility of having stained-glass windows in the church. He told them that the church could not afford to have stained-glass windows, but they still insisted that there must be some way. He asked if I would meet with them and explain how time-consuming and how expensive stained-glass windows would be, so maybe then they would give up the idea.

Before I met with the committee, I made a small sample of stained glass depicting Jesus to demonstrate the difficulty and time involved and the expense of the glass. When I passed the piece around at the meeting, I realized that they were not listening to me. They were visualizing the piece of glass in one of their windows.

By the time I left the church that evening, I had committed myself to design, make, and install twenty-four large, stained-glass windows at no expense to the church!

> "Faith, mighty faith,
> the promise sees.
> And looks to God alone;
> Laughs at impossibilities,
> And cries it shall be done."
> —Charles Wesley

On the way home, I looked up and said, "God, what have you gotten me into?" It was perfectly clear to me that the promise I had made years before during the flying event was ready to be fulfilled.

The first thing I had to do when I got home was to put an extension on my work table to handle four-by-eight-foot-wide stained-glass windows. Next, I had to get a copy of a children's Bible, not only to learn the stories of the Bible but to get some ideas for the pictures I would be making with small pieces of stained glass.

Trinity Hill Methodist Church had six windows at the top of each of the four walls. The windows were four feet tall and eight feet wide, which was an awkward size for church windows. When I made the initial sketches of the first six windows, the effect looked like a comic strip.

Being from the Southwest, I always loved arched windows, so I created the pictures in a large arch with a light blue background. The effect was more effective than I had visualized. The stories seemed to flow from one to the next, from left to right around the room.

I borrowed heavily from the children's Bible; I didn't want anyone who saw the windows to not know which Bible story was being told. I hoped they would be encouraged to find out more about the stories.

As I completed each window, I placed it in a frame I made from one-by-four boards around the outside and a sheet of four-by-eight-foot, thin plywood sheets, with one on top and the other on the bottom. The sheets of plywood were bolted to the frame with short bolts and wing nuts. With high scaffolds, we were able to lift the stained-glass windows up to the bottom of the existing windows, unbolt the top piece of plywood, and then place the stained-glass windows against the existing window.

I thought we were finished when the twenty-fourth window was installed in the sanctuary, but Shirley thought we should have a large window of Leonardo da Vinci's *The Last Supper* in the narthex. God must have been working again. Even though I felt a strong communication with God, I admit that I still didn't feel a closeness with Jesus. But the last pieces of glass I fitted into *The Last Supper* were the hands of Jesus. Something wonderful happened. I didn't hear anything with my ears, but in my heart, I heard him say, "Good job." We will always be close now.

The evening after we installed *The Last Supper*, I was driving home and looked up and said, "OK, now we are even."

When I got home, I had a message to call a woman who was the pastor of a small Methodist church in Frankfort, Kentucky. I called her and she said, "Doctor Canady, I heard about your ministry and I wonder if you would consider doing the windows for our church."

I told her I would look at her church the next day, and after I hung up, I said, "OK, we're not even yet."

By the time I had finished the windows for the church in Frankfort, Shirley had been selected as president of the University of Memphis and a new chapter was beginning.

Stained-Glass Ministry Partnership

After Dr. Canady arrived in Memphis and word got out that he was a stained-glass artist, many churches approached him to created stained-glass windows for them. Bob decided that he would only design, create, and install stained-glass windows for churches that could not afford it. Other churches could pay stained-glass artists, but he did not want to take work from the artists who created stained glass for a living, so he did the work without compensation.

Photo by Mark Stansbury

Dr. Canady created stained-glass windows for many churches in and around Memphis, including Freedom's Chapel Christian Church, Disciples of Christ.

Dr. Canady and Mark Stansbury, executive assistant for community relations for University of Memphis President Shirley Raines's office, formed a partnership to identify, visit with pastors, and begin a stained-glass ministry in Memphis and the surrounding areas. Without Mark Stansbury's assistance, Bob's stained-glass ministry in and around Memphis would not have been possible.

Wright's Chapel was the first church identified by the Canady-Stansbury partnership.

—*Dr. Shirley Raines*

From the Canady Photo Collection

Photo above: Dr. Robert Canady and his wife, Dr. Shirley Raines, took this photo together at their home in Oak Ridge, Tennessee.

Photo at left: Dr. Robert Canady is seated in front of the Grove Park Inn in Asheville, North Carolina.

Photo by Dr. Shirley Raines

Photo from the University of Memphis Magazine photography

Dr. Bob Canady, first man, and Dr. Shirley Raines, president of the University of Memphis, ride in the Homecoming Parade in 2013.

21
From Lexington to Memphis

S hirley was not only the first woman to serve as president of the University of Memphis, but she became one of the most respected presidents to serve in Memphis and the state of Tennessee.

My story of the twelve years we were in Memphis is told from the perspective of the president's spouse. Shirley has documented her story in her wonderful book, *An Uncommon Journey: From Preschool Teacher to University President.*

In my retirement, I have tried to support Shirley when I could by attending many social events and giving her my expert opinions concerning important matters.

For instance, when I learned about the position of dean of the College of Education at the University of Kentucky, I advised her to apply. When she was nominated for the position at the University of Memphis, I was quick with my expert advice. I told her, "They will never hire a woman as president of the University of Memphis."

When she became a finalist, I was there again for her, so she would not be disappointed. I said, "Shirley, they always make sure they have a woman in their final pool of applicants, but you know, there are few women presidents at universities in Tennessee, except at community colleges. This is a university."

Shirley became the eleventh president and the first woman to be named president in the university's over 100 years of existence.

Before we even moved to Memphis, Shirley got even with me for giving her my wonderful advice. After she was selected as president, one committee member said, "You do play golf, don't you?" (All presidents are expected to play golf.)

Without a pause, Shirley said, "No, but Bob will."

> "If you watch a game, it's fun. If you play a game, it's recreation. If you work at it, it's golf."
> —Bob Hope

I had never played golf in my life, and I told Shirley that I was too old to learn. She said, "Well, I told them you would." So I went to Walmart and bought one of every kind of club, everything for about a hundred dollars. I went to a nearby golf range, found a spot away from the "real golfers," and started to try to make contact with the ball. To my surprise, I did better than I expected, but the ball always curved off to the right.

A young man who had been watching me said, "Mind if I make a suggestion?"

I said, "Please do." He corrected my swing, and I decided that after some lessons, I might learn to play golf.

Shortly afterward, we moved to the university-owned president's house in Memphis. The athletic director called me and said, "Bob, bring your clubs with you to the faculty retreat. You are signed up to play in the golf tournament." I told him that was impossible. I was still trying to make contact with the ball. He told me not to worry because no one took the tournament seriously.

The three men who played with me were very kind, and I managed to make it around the course. After dinner that evening, various awards were given for categories such as "longest drive," "closest to the pin," and "lowest score." Then they called my name. I reluctantly went to the front of the room and the presenter said, "Bob, here are a dozen golf balls. We know it won't pay up for all the ones you lost, but we wanted you to have them."

I soon learned that the people at the university really did play golf for fun, although some of them also used golf as a means of giving advice concerning administrative matters at the university. The advice was often introduced by the comment, "Now, don't tell Shirley, but I think she should . . ."

Golf soon became one of my favorite pastimes. I still play and enjoy it if I don't keep score.

I found that being the husband of the first woman president of the University of Memphis was a unique experience for all concerned. Everyone was eager to make sure the spouse was happy, and they were relieved to learn that I would be spending most of my free time involved in my various art interests, especially my stained-glass projects.

> "Golf is a good walk spoiled."
> —Mark Twain
>
> "Golf is a game in which you yell 'fore,' shoot six, and write down five."
> —Paul Harvey

When we were first shown the president's house, which was near the university, Shirley said, "It is beautiful, but there is no place for Bob to do his stained-glass art."

The head of the maintenance department said, "There is a building out in the back that was once used as a recording studio that you might like to look at."

We walked to the back to find a garage-sized brick building with large windows facing the south. When we entered the building, the maintenance man started apologizing for the condition inside. He said the walls had been lined with soundproofing materials, which had been removed and exposed the bare studs, and most of the light fixtures had been removed.

To me, I only saw an art studio that I had always dreamed of. It even had a bathroom.

When I told the maintenance man how perfect it was, he said that of course they would finish the walls and add anything I needed. He was obviously relieved and quickly removed a notebook from his pocket and began making a list of everything I needed for a perfect art studio.

> "The only time my prayers are never answered is on the golf course."
> —Billy Graham

When we were leaving the art studio to return to the main house, he asked if I was sure I didn't need anything else. I told him I couldn't think of anything.

Then he quickly said, "How about a TV hookup?"

And I said, "Of course, every art studio needs a TV."

The news of my "stained-glass church window ministry" soon spread throughout the university and the city of Memphis. Mark Stansbury, a member of Shirley's staff, was particularly interested. Mark was a longtime member of the community; a part-time deejay for WDIA, an African-American-owned radio station; and a respected community leader. He wanted to speak with me about a Black church that was in dire need of a stained-glass window at their church entrance. He assured me there was no way the church could afford to pay for the window.

I agreed to accompany Mark to see the church, which was located northeast of Memphis. When I visualized the window at the church entrance, it seemed to transform the whole church. I knew I had to do it. I also knew that my "debt" to God wasn't even near being paid.

When we left the church, I realized that because of my new relationship with Mark, who is African-American, my life was about to make another important change.

Photos by Mark Stansbury

'Enter to Worship, Depart to Serve,' says the stained-glass window above the front doors of Wright's Chapel AME Church in Arlington, Tennessee. The window was designed and created by Dr. Robert Canady. The pastor was Rev. Walter Cox, now deceased.

Wright's Chapel AME Church was the first church in the Memphis area where Dr. Canady designed windows.

Photos from the Canady Photo Collection
The 'Southern Roots' show with Dr. Canady aired in July 2007.

Photo above: Dr. Canady is interviewed for 'Southern Roots' about his stained-glass ministry. Photo at left: The interview took place in his studio behind the University of Memphis president's residence, where he and Dr. Raines lived during her time as president from 2001 to 2013.

Photos from the Canady Photo Collection

Photo courtesy of the University of Memphis

Dr. Bob Canady and Dr. Shirley Raines attend the University of Memphis Law School Gala in 2010.

From the Canady Photo Collection

This photo was taken in 2023 and is one of the last photos of Bob at the University of Memphis.

Cairo Baptist Church Stained Glass

According to church member Shelby Raines, Cairo Baptist Church was founded in 1910 and met in the Cairo School across the road from the present church until a building could be constructed. The church is located in a rural area of Crockett County, near Alamo, Tennessee. Brother Bill Robbins was the pastor when Dr. Canady created and installed the first set of windows. Brother Bob Dennison was the pastor when the church burned and during the rebuild. Dr. Canady rebuilt the windows for the reconstructed church, and they were dedicated in October of 2017.

Deacon Carey Raines and other church leaders were intricately involved with Dr. Canady in selecting the themes for the first set of windows. After the church burned, Bob generously created and donated a second set of windows with many of the same designs.

The story of the Cairo angel emanates from the attempt to save any of the first set of windows after the church burned, thought to be from faulty electrical wiring. Heartbroken, Dr. Canady and church members combed through the windows, charred and broken from the intense fire, but they thought nothing could be saved. Unwilling to give up, Bob took the window with the angel home with him to Oak Ridge. Using oven cleaner, he attempted to save the angel window. The glass was splintered and cracked. One piece, the angel in the center, was the only thing he could rescue from the fire.

After creating, installing, and dedicating the new windows for the rebuilt church, Bob saw one smaller window that was an exit door near the front right side of the sanctuary and decided to create one more stained-glass window for Cairo Baptist Church. He designed a special window with the angel, which the church members began to call the Cairo angel, as a symbol of the resurrection of the church building and of hope for their lives.

—*Dr. Shirley Raines and Shelby Raines*

Canady Stained-Glass Windows for Cairo Baptist Church near Alamo, Tennessee

Canady Stained-Glass Windows for Cairo Baptist Church near Alamo, Tennessee

Photos by Mark Stansbury

Dr. Canady created stained-glass windows depicting creation (left), baby Jesus (center), and the Communion of wine and bread (right) for Greater Payne Chapel African Methodist Episcopal Church in Memphis, Tennessee, where Rev. Quinten L. Smith is the pastor.

22
Respect, Honesty, and Race

I spent most of my early years in New Mexico, Arizona, and California. Since the racial problems with African Americans seemed to me to be mostly in the South, I didn't pay a lot of attention to their problems. I didn't encounter many racial problems in the Air Force, and even while at the University of Alabama, I spent most of my time at the university and, unfortunately, ignored the racial problems that existed.

While in Oklahoma, we learned more about the Cherokees. We enjoyed working with the teachers, and we were fortunate to talk with leaders in the Cherokee Nation headquartered in Tahlequah. I knew more about Native American people because my grandfather had a wife who was Cherokee; however, we had no verification, only stories. Often, the Cherokee people in Oklahoma laughed because it seems that many of the mostly white people who visit them at the headquarters now claim to have Cherokee blood. However, during my childhood, it was never mentioned. I was a teenager when my uncle, who had darker skin and features, came to visit and I found out more about my grandfather and one of his wives. Later in Tucson at the University of Arizona, I taught some classes on the Navajo Reservation.

While my own Cherokee ancestry, experiences in New Mexico and Arizona, and Air Force assignments were quite limited, Mark Stansbury became my educator.

Mark had lived through the horrors of racial discrimination in Memphis and was still able to believe in the good in people and share his faith in God. I told Mark about my talk with Nat King Cole when I was a page at the NBC Studio, and even as a star, Mr. Cole experienced harsh discrimination. He was not allowed to stay in many of the fancy hotels where he was the star of the show.

> "The secret of a good sermon is to have a good beginning and a good ending, then having the two as close together as possible."
> —George Burns

What made my relationship special with Mark was that we preferred to express our faith in action, not words.

Mark knew that I only created the windows for churches that couldn't possibly afford to pay for them. It was important to me that stained-glass artists who needed to make a living should get the commissions from churches that could afford them.

While in Memphis, I designed, created, and installed stained-glass windows for thirteen churches. Eight were primarily Black churches, which Mark helped me choose. Shirley and I, along with Mark and his wife, Imogene, always looked forward to the dedication services at the Black churches because of the wonderful sermons and the music.

Two services were especially memorable. When the dedication for the first church was planned, I told the minister that several faculty members from the University of Memphis asked if they could attend, and, of course, the minister said they were welcome.

On the Sunday of the dedication, several members of the faculty attended, and the minister gave them a warm welcome. Then he said, "By the way, all you white people who think you're going to get out of here at twelve o'clock, forget it."

His comment brought down the house, and everyone enjoyed a great long sermon, beautiful music, and afterward a delicious lunch of Southern food, including some soul-food specialties.

During another dedication at an African-American church, Shirley and I sat in front and enjoyed the enthusiastic preaching and wonderful choir. At the end of the service, Shirley was given a beautiful bouquet of flowers, and I was given a plaque. As we stood to leave, the minister said, "Sit down. We aren't through yet." The area bishop, who had a wonderful baritone voice, sang a beautiful religious hymn, but he changed the words to fit the stained-glass windows. The last words of the song were changed to "Thank God for these beautiful windows and thank God for Dr. Bob." Shirley and I both had tears in our eyes.

When I'm asked for how many churches I have provided the stained-glass windows, I reply, "Fourteen." The thirteenth church and the fourteenth are the same church. It was a small church, Cairo Baptist Church, out in the country near where Shirley grew up and which her brother attended in Alamo, Tennessee.

> "I get one hour, really twenty-five minutes in a sermon on a weekend, to combat all the hours of the week that people are told you are what you have through billboards, commercials, and sitcoms, and so forth."
>
> —Max Lucado

The building had been destroyed by fire, and the congregation was devastated by the loss of the windows. I assured them that if they could raise enough money to rebuild the building, I would redo the windows. I asked if any of the glass had survived, hoping I could use some of it. I was told that they had stacked what was left of the windows behind the site where the church had burned. The glass was totally smoked black on both sides, and they couldn't tell if any of it was usable.

I went to the church site and found large shards of some of the windows still intact. I took them home, and Shirley and I placed them on the cement driveway at our house and used oven cleaner and steel wool to clean them, only to find out that there were small cracks in most of the pieces. The fire had been so hot that most of the solder had melted.

The congregation had been so pleased with the original windows that I made the new ones the same as the old ones. After I installed them, the congregation, including Shirley's brother and sister-in-law, Carey and Shelby, were thrilled. When I realized there was a small window on the outside door near the front of the sanctuary that had no stained glass, we rectified that so that the entire sanctuary had stained-glass windows.

Much later, I received a call from a deacon of an old Methodist church near the church I had redone. The beautiful old building developed structural problems, and when the brick wall at the back of the sanctuary cracked, three of the old stained-glass windows were damaged. I first told him I didn't do repair work because I had found that it was not possible to find matching glass and because the old lead channeling that holds the glass is corroded and the new solder won't stick to it.

> "Darkness cannot drive out darkness; only light can do that. Hate cannot drive out hate; only love can do that."
> —Dr. Martin Luther King Jr.

Like a true Methodist, the deacon wouldn't give up. He said he would like to bring the windows to me and see what I could do.

After twelve years, Shirley had retired from the University of Memphis and we had moved to Oak Ridge, which is a five-hour drive away. I told him that if he was willing to make that drive, I would look at them. We agreed that he would drive over on a good day and we planned to meet on Interstate 40 at the turn-off to Oak Ridge.

He called when it was near the time we were to meet, and I realized he was not even halfway to Oak Ridge. Finally, I received a second call, and the man and his wife were waiting at a gas station at the turn-off to Oak Ridge. I asked how I would recognize him, and he said, "Oh, you'll recognize me all right!"

When Shirley and I turned into the gas station, over to one side on a small patch of grass was an elderly man sitting with his shirt unbuttoned, looking totally exhausted. Next to him was a small car that had seen better days. The back windows had been rolled down, and protruding from each window was about two feet of what obviously were some very old stained-glass windows.

I asked him if he was really driving on the interstate like that, and he said, "It would have been all right, but you have to drive so blamed fast, the car kept trying to take off!"

His wife came out of the gas station, where she had been trying to recuperate, and she also was exhausted.

They followed us to our house, where we unloaded the windows and put them in my studio downstairs. We invited them to spend the night and get some rest, but the man insisted they needed to get back home.

Shirley asked if they were going back on the interstate, and he said, "I'd walk before I'd get on that thing again!"

He got out a map and said they had found a way to get home through small towns and they planned to take their time and stop at each town if they wanted.

The windows turned out to be more of a carpentry project than a stained-glass one. I was able to replace the broken pieces with glass that was a close match, and I refinished the wood frames surrounding the window.

When I finished, I called and he informed me that the wall of the church had been repaired. They were ready for the windows. When I told the man who had delivered the windows that I would bring the windows to them, he said, "I thought you were a saint, and now I know it."

When I carried the windows into the church and saw them on the back wall, it was like bringing that beautiful old church back to life. I imagined a warm smile from God.

The old church was in a community close to where I had installed the windows for the church that burned. I decided to stop by there to see the windows again. I was surprised to see one of the men working at the church who had helped install the new windows.

He said he had found a smaller window that had been in the entrance to the church that burned. He brought it out, and it was completely covered with black on both sides. We couldn't tell what condition it was in, but I told him I would take it home and clean it.

When I brought it home and finally managed to get it clean, I realized it was a smaller version of the design on the larger windows. There was a stylized cross with a beautiful angel in the center. I was so happy about how the angel looked that I wanted to put it at the entrance to the church.

I quickly called the church to determine the size of the glass on the new door at the side of the front of the sanctuary. We measured the new window. I was pleased to learn that I could trim the stained glass a little bit all the way around. It fit into the new door perfectly.

The first Sunday after the window was installed, several church members commented that "she" wouldn't give up that easily. Now, "she," the angel, is back where she belongs.

Photo by Mark Stansbury

Dr. Canady created a Holy Bible stained-glass window for Greater Payne Chapel AME Church in Memphis, Tennessee. Rev. Quinten L. Smith is the pastor.

Photo by Mark Stansbury

Dr. Canady and the Rev. Dr. Rosalyn Nichols attend the dedication for the windows at Freedom's Chapel Christian Church, Disciples of Christ.

From left: Mark Stansbury, Dr. Shirley Raines, national civil rights leader Dr. Maxine Smith, and Dr. Bob Canady at Freedom's Chapel Christian Church, Disciples of Christ.

From the Canady Photo Collection

Stained-Glass Lamps

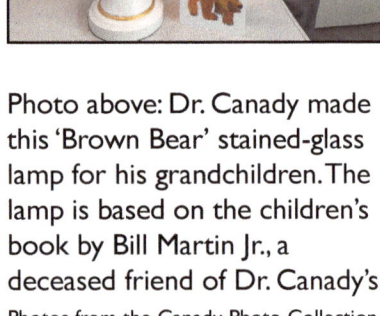

Photo above: Dr. Canady made this 'Brown Bear' stained-glass lamp for his grandchildren. The lamp is based on the children's book by Bill Martin Jr., a deceased friend of Dr. Canady's.
Photos from the Canady Photo Collection

Photo at left: Dianne Papasan, Le Bonheur Children's Hospital curator of art, bought this lamp at a charity auction.

Stained-Glass Lamps

Photos from the Canady Photo Collection

Dr. Canady presents a stained-glass lamp to artist and friend Dr. Ann Brown, MD. At left is his wife, Dr. Shirley Raines. Dr. Canady has given away most of his lamps to nonprofits for fundraising.

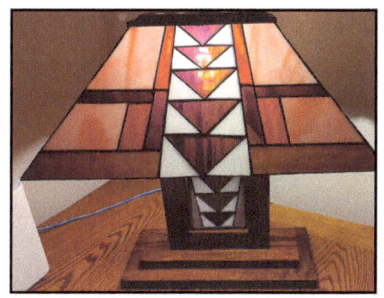

First United Methodist Church

Fire swept through the historic downtown First United Methodist Church in Memphis on October 6, 2006.

The church, which was built in 1893, was largely destroyed by the flames. Its roof caved in, the steeple toppled, and some of the walls crumbled onto the streets.

The fire started before four in the morning in the basement of First United Methodist Church and quickly spread through the church sanctuary.

Rev. Martha Wagley was the pastor. Dr. Canady called her and volunteered to create some stained-glass windows. Since it would be quite some time before the main building was rebuilt, he designed three stained-glass windows for the chapel.

Rev. Wagley was called by the fire department at 3:15 a.m. Dr. Canady placed that time on the clock tower. This window is one of three that are associated with the history of the Methodist church.
—*Dr. Shirley Raines*

From the Canady Photo Collection

Dr. Canady created this stained-glass window for First United Methodist Church in Memphis.

From the Canady Photo Collection

Dr. Canady created this stained-glass window for First United Methodist Church, which was rebuilt after a fire destroyed much of the historic downtown Memphis landmark.

From the Canady Photo Collection

The pastor of Friendship United Methodist Church in Millington, Tennessee, was Cynthia Davis.

From the Canady Photo Collection

The stained-glass windows above were installed and created by Dr. Canady for Friendship United Methodist Church in Millington, Tennessee, in 2007.

Photo by Mark Stansbury

Dr. Shirley Raines, Dr. Bob Canady, and Imogene Stansbury gather to attend the stained-glass window dedication at Greater Payne Chapel African Methodist Episcopal Church in Memphis, Tennessee. Rev. Quinten L. Smith is the pastor.

Photo by Mark Stansbury

Dr. Canady stands on a ladder measuring for a stained-glass window for Greater Payne Chapel AME Church.

From the Canady Photo Collection

Mark Stansbury, photographer, is pictured with his wife, Imogene, a talented soloist who is well-known in the Memphis area and was often invited to sing when the stained-glass windows were dedicated.

From the Canady Photo Collection

Dr. Canady with Pastor Shirley Prince, now deceased, who was the founder and pastor of Philippians V Multi-Ministry Center in Memphis, Tennessee.

23
The Artist and My Right Brain

Through the years, I probably made a hundred stained-glass lamps, and I never made the same design twice. Most were given to charity auctions to support worthy causes. Some lamps were given to friends, and several are in our home.

It is the same with painting. When I design a lamp or paint a picture, I have an idea of what to do, but I just relax and let the ideas come to me. I never feel closer to God than when I am involved in the creative process.

As I mentioned earlier in my stories, it wasn't until I was involved in my doctoral program that I learned the main reason for my difficulties in school was that I was a right-brained learner in mostly left-brain educational programs. Once I understood that, I learned to compensate by forming visual images to help me remember the material at test time. I could get the right answer many times without understanding the concept.

As a university professor, I was successful because I used visual aids in every class, not only to help the students but to organize the materials I was presenting. I was a full professor at the time I retired and still in demand for speaking engagements throughout the country.

My fans would have been shocked to learn that I couldn't type or use a computer. Technology had completely passed by this extremely right-brained learner.

Shirley is still amazed that I flew airplanes all over the country with very limited knowledge concerning the technical part of flying, a limited knowledge that almost cost me my life!

I've given some examples of what it is like for an extremely right-brained person to live in a predominantly left-brain world, but how does all of that relate to religion?

> "To fall in love with God is the greatest romance; to seek him is the greatest adventure; to find him is the greatest human achievement."
> —Saint Augustine

After I learned that the picture of an angry God that scared me as a child was really a picture of Moses, I created a picture in my mind of God in a white robe floating around in the sky and "keeping score" of every individual on Earth. When each person died, God checked the person's score, and the ones who passed went to Heaven and the ones who failed went to Hell. Of course, the ones who had gone to church received extra credit.

Later, when I was older, I asked why I couldn't see God. I was told that we can't see the wind, either, but we know it's there. That analogy became critical for my religious belief for most of my life. I realized that most of religion is based on faith. You don't have to see it to believe it.

As I stated earlier, to please Shirley, I started attending church for the first time in my life as an adult. I soon learned that the highlights of the services for me in our Alabama church were Alabama football jokes. I asked Shirley if people really believed in all the miracles that are in the Bible. She told me that they have faith in what the Bible meant. I didn't say it, but I thought it was much easier to have faith in the wind.

Many years ago, while I was still trying to be an actor, I won an award for my role as Henry Drummond in the famous play *Inherit the Wind*. To prepare for the part, I reread Charles Darwin's book on evolution. I'll never forget the feeling I had in the last scene of the play. I picked up a copy of Darwin's book in one hand and the Bible in the other. After a short pause, I put the two books together, put them in my briefcase, and left the stage.

I don't believe that God is a man or a woman. I believe that God is a power—a power so strong that we can't really comprehend it, a power strong enough to create everything that exists. We now know that all matter, including the human body, can be broken down into individual elements, and those elements can be identified.

My belief is that this powerful God created the earth in a way that it would support life and then put all of the elements necessary to create life on Earth. God knew that if life was to survive on Earth, then all life had to be creative.

Time has no meaning to God; therefore, the billions of years that it took for the elements of life to come together weren't important. What was important was that new life was created. I strongly agree that God created the heavens and the earth and all the living things, but I don't believe children should be told that it was done in seven days.

Without the Bible, Christianity would not exist, and it will always be the foundation of Christian belief. For our children and people like me, the stories must have relevance to their personal lives.

Through the years, Shirley and I have been fortunate to find pastors who are able to read a passage directly from the Bible and then retell the story in a clever or poignant way that leaves no doubt about the relevance of the Bible passage to life.

One Sunday morning, when Shirley and I went to our church in Oak Ridge, we listened to another wonderful sermon. Our pastor never used the pulpit. He read from the Bible, which is on a podium on one side of the stage, and then moved back and forth, almost acting out the passage.

Other than reading an illustrated children's Bible to get ideas for the twenty-four stained-glass windows for the first church in Lexington, I had never actually read the Bible. The stories didn't make sense to me.

Now I check the bulletin that we receive in the mail each week to see which passage the minister will use next Sunday in his sermon. I even try to anticipate what clever ways he will choose to retell a Bible passage in a way to relate to our personal lives. I especially like the way he deals with the miracles in the Bible. He has no doubt that a God who can create the universe and all that exists is capable of parting a sea, feeding thousands with a few loaves of bread, or even performing immaculate conception, but he knows how difficult it is for those of us with no religious background to accept those miracles out of our faith in God.

Our pastor refuses to let non-believers dismiss the miracles as pure fantasy by stressing the message the Bible story has for our personal lives, whether or not we believe the miracle took place as described in the passage. Being an extremely right-brained person, I only learn what I can visualize. "I see, therefore I am."

What really happened that day when I survived what appeared to be certain death in a small airplane returning from Canada?

I have spent many hours since that event trying to understand how and what happened. The easy answer is that God intervened and directed me to an airport. Even though I'm sure God has the power to do that, I don't believe that is what happened.

I believe that when God created the earth with all the elements and forces necessary for life, the most important force was creativity. All life depended on creative ability to exist and survive.

Being raised in an environment where religion was only discussed in negative terms, I had no concept of the Bible's version of the beginning of life on Earth. Most of what I heard from friends only confused me. It sounded like a fairy tale. It wasn't until I was introduced to the theory of evolution that I thought seriously about how it all happened.

What fascinated me the most was that humans were given the power of creative thought.

Now I realize that God planned for humans to use their creative abilities to ensure the survival of the earth.

Once I stopped being concerned about whether the incidents in the Bible stories happened exactly as they are written and began to pay more attention to the important messages they contained, the Bible and the sermons had more meaning for me. There is no doubt that God, who can create everything that exists, can also perform the miracles referred to in the Bible.

Back to my flying incident. I now believe that God certainly has the power to intervene and direct me to an airport, but I don't believe that is what happens when we call on God. The Holy Spirit within me told me to stop panicking and use my creative mind. That was when I remembered the interstate and the way out of the valley. Seeing the runway seconds before I was losing all visibility—that was God's intervention, His "amazing grace."

I have told this story to the congregations of fifteen churches and to several Sunday school classes, and it was shown on statewide public television and appeared in several newspapers. I hope the story has caused other doubters to take a closer look at their own religious questions and beliefs.

Dr. Canady created a stained-glass window in the ceiling for a church in the round, St. Paul's United Methodist Church in Frankfort, Kentucky. The pastor is Rev. Marcia Woodward.
From the Canady Photo Collection

Photo above: Dr. Bob Canady works on a stained-glass window installation at Trinity Hill Methodist Church in Lexington, Kentucky, with two church members. Photo at right: Bob's hands insert Jesus's hands into the *Last Supper* stained-glass window, which Bob created for Trinity Hill Methodist Church in Lexington, Kentucky, in 1997.
Photos from the Canady Photo Collection

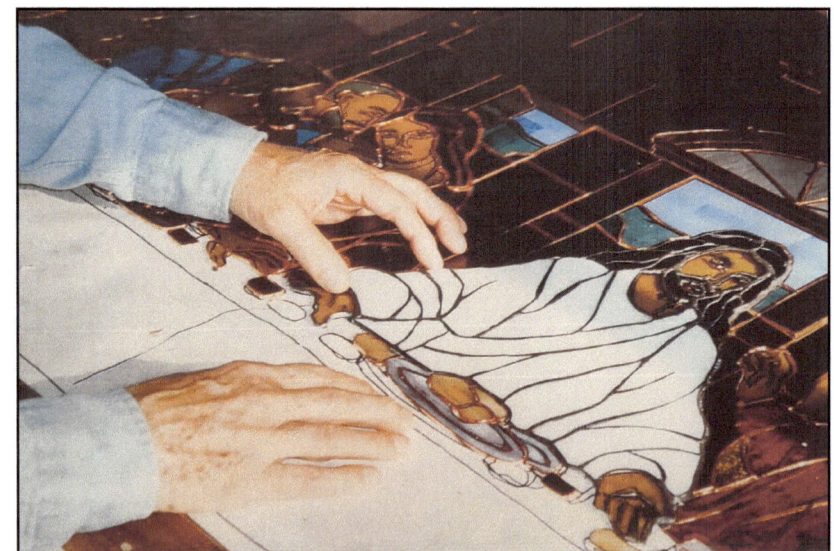

From the Canady Photo Collection

Dr. Shirley Raines wrote a book about bees that is featured on the Nature Book Trail with large posters of the pages of the book posted across the hillside and along the trail. Dr Canady enjoyed sitting on the bench with the *Bees* photo.

Photo by Brian Smith

Dr. Robert Canady and his wife, Dr. Shirley Raines, retired to Oak Ridge, Tennessee.

About the Author

Dr. Robert Canady is a retired educator who served in the Air Force during the Korean War, and he attended college first on a football scholarship and later on the GI Bill. His talents as an artist were discovered early in his life, and he has always said that colleges like artists who play football.

Because Dr. Canady grew up poor in Hurley, New Mexico, he didn't have the benefit of a strong early education. That fueled his determination that he would teach children better ways to learn to read. Before he achieved his doctorate, he worked in Hollywood as an aspiring actor. Later, he founded a Montessori school in Santa Barbara, California.

For many years, Dr. Canady flew his private plane around the United States until, one day, he nearly crashed during a violent storm. He thanked God for saving his life, and he soon found a new ministry—creating stained-glass windows for churches that couldn't afford them.

Along the way, he met and married Dr. Shirley Raines, who became the University of Memphis's first female president. Dr. Canady and Dr. Raines collaborated on three books:

■ Raines, S. C. & Canady, R. J. (1989). *Story S-t-r-e-t-c-h-e-r-s: Activities to Expand Children's Favorite Books*. Mt. Rainier, MD: Gryphon House.

■ Raines, S. C. & Canady, R. J. (1990). *The Whole Language Kindergarten*. Foreword by Bill Martin Jr.: New York: Teachers College, Columbia University.

■ Raines, S. C. & Canady, R. J. (1992). *Story S-t-r-e-t-c-h-e-r-s for the Primary Grades: Activities to Expand Children's Favorite Books*. Mt. Rainier, MD: Gryphon House.

Although Dr. Canady has written many educational papers and books, he always wanted to write his *Life Stories*.

From the Canady Photo Collection

Dr. Canady created this stained-glass window for Friendship United Methodist Church in Millington, Tennessee. In the Greek alphabet, in which the New Testament was written, alpha is the first letter and omega is the last. In the Book of Revelation, God says, 'I am Alpha and Omega, the first and the last,' meaning that God remains from the beginning to the end of time.

www.ingramcontent.com/pod-product-compliance
Lightning Source LLC
Chambersburg PA
CBHW051513110526
44582CB00008B/149